Re-Visioning Retirement

— A Workbook —

RE-VISIONING RETIREMENT

— A WORKBOOK —

What's next?

What do I aspire to?

What's my legacy?

SUSAN REID, PHD

BARLOW BOOKS
fine books for enterprising authors

Copyright © Susan Reid, 2025
Illustrations by Gillian Reid

All rights reserved, including those for data and text mining, AI training, and similar technologies. No part of this publication may be reproduced, stored in a retrieval system or transmitted, in any form or by any means, without prior written consent of the publisher.

Library and Archives Canada Cataloguing in Publication data available upon request.

ISBN 978-1-998841-17-2

Printed in Canada

Publisher: Sarah Scott
Book producer: Tracy Bordian/At Large Editorial Services
Editor: Eleanor Gasparik
Copy editor: Dawn Loewen
Interior design and layout: Rob Scanlan

For more information, visit **www.barlowbooks.com**

Barlow Book Publishing Inc.
96 Elm Avenue, Toronto, ON
Canada M4W 1P2

*For the visionaries who inspire us
to be true to our calling*

Contents

Introduction: So This Is Retirement... 1

THE POWER OF VISION 11
What Is Vision? 11
Why Is Vision Important? 18
Why Is Re-Visioning Retirement Important? 25
The FUN Re-Visioning Process:
   Foundations, Uncovering, Nurturing 33
How to Use This Workbook:
   Your Road Map to FUN Re-Visioning 34
Try This Prep Exercise 40

PILLAR 1: FOUNDATIONS (WEEK 1) 45
Your Authentic Self 45
Exercise 1. Embrace Your Authentic Self: Values 47
Exercise 2. Embrace Your Authentic Self:
   Skills and Learning Styles 60
Exercise 3. Embrace Your Authentic Self: Passions ... 64
Exercise 4. Explore Your Authentic Self 67
Exercise 5. Deepen Your Authentic Self 70

BREAK FOR PERSONAL REFLECTION 74

PILLAR 2: UNCOVERING (WEEK 2) — 79
- Your Aspirational Self — 79
- Exercise 6. Discover Aspirational Values — 82
- Exercise 7. Name It — 86
- Exercise 8. Activate: Attitude — 90
- Exercise 9. Activate: Alignment — 94
- Exercise 10. Activate: Amplification — 103

BREAK FOR GUIDED REFLECTION — 108

PILLAR 3: NURTURING (WEEK 3) — 127
- Your Visionary Self — 127
- Three Strategies for Constructing a Vision Statement — 129
- Exercise 11. Define Your Vision Goal — 131
- Exercise 12. Draft Your Core Message — 137
- Exercise 13. Bring Your Vision into Focus — 140
- Exercise 14. Create Your Vision Statement — 147
- Exercise 15. Lay Down Your First Stepping Stone — 152

Enjoy the Journey! — 157
Endnotes — 160
Acknowledgements — 167

INTRODUCTION
So This Is Retirement...

EXPERIENCING THAT LONG-AWAITED TRIP, taking a beat to enjoy some self-reflection and journalling in your diary, having fun with your besties ... and just press the repeat button for the rest of time. Sounds pretty good, right?

Taking time out to relax and not having to plan your days too much is a great kickoff to retirement. But the desire to get back to "normal" can start to set in. You may start to sense this gradually, or it can hit you all at once. For me, it happened in 2021, right at the end of my three-week post-retirement trip...

I had the first panic attack of my 57-year-old life.

I was deep in the dairy section of a supersize grocery store in the middle of France, deciding between a round of Brie and a hunk of Camembert. All of a sudden, my breathing got shallow, and I felt dizzy. Before I knew it, the cheeses and I were splayed across the floor. When I came to, I knew exactly what it was about, too: the reality that I was returning home with absolutely no plan for my future. I'd gone from pedal-to-the-metal work to zilch in the blink of an eye.

The month prior, I had taken early retirement from my career as a tenured professor in marketing and entrepreneurship at the Williams School of Business, Bishop's University,

Canada. There had been an online goodbye party with my university colleagues, a lovely gift from the business school, and a mention in the year-end principal's address. There had been dinner festivities with friends and family and kind words of thanks from previous students. And then, there had been the plan to go to Europe to relax and enjoy.

What there had *not* been was a retirement plan.

Like so many of us entering "retirement"—which the *Cambridge Dictionary*, and I kid you not, defines as "the act of leaving your job and stopping working, usually because you are old"[1]—I had not given any real thought to what my retirement might even look like.

The irony? The main focus of my academic research and career over the past three decades had been VISION—what it is, why it's important, and how to create it. And yet here I was, with no vision whatsoever for my own retirement.

I also realized that I was not alone! There are currently some 1.4 billion "retirement-age" (65+) people in developed and developing countries, and with this number predicted to double by 2050,[2] there's never before been such a need for guidance at this stage of life.

And here's the kicker: Based on the research I've done, most of these people are like me—they don't have a vision or a plan for their retirement either! But what I *do* have in my back pocket is this: I have a step-by-step process for creating a vision.

I know from experience, and from my own research in the business world, that vision can guide professional endeavours in a way that's more likely to achieve success. I quickly realized that this would also likely apply to figuring out what to do in retirement. Let's take a closer look.

INTRODUCING THE NEW RETIREES

The nature of retirement has changed dramatically during the last half century. Back when my parents retired in the late 1980s, the average retirement age was 65. Fast forward a few decades and my husband and I were both retired by the age of 60—we were confirmed "Freedom 55ers"!

My husband and I are part of an increasingly common trend, too: early retirement.[3] Early retirement simply means leaving an established "mid- or late-stage career before mandatory retirement age."[4] And as the age of first retirement (from one's main work-life chapter) continues to decrease, retirement ceases to follow the old rules and starts looking more like the newly and appropriately named "Great Resignation."[5] Also known as the "Big Quit," this was not a phenomenon of the pandemic—nope, it's been at play for more than a decade.[6]

And the trend is continuing. Our children, now in their 20s, and many of their friends (particularly those from Gen Z)[7] are increasingly hoping to pocket enough money from their first jobs to "retire" in their 40s or 50s—or earlier. And after that, preferably, do something on their own not involving working for "the man." Some are even considering "mini-retirements" or adult gap years, using them to travel or pursue other projects.

So, if the trend toward living longer continues, with coming generations predicted to live well into their 100s,[8] the question becomes: What are we going to do with so much time—and perhaps not enough money—on our hands?

ENTER: RE-VISIONING RETIREMENT

As we transition from the goals we set that took us through school, early careers, and relationships into our midlife, we may notice that some of the values which originally drove those goals have shifted, or we may desire them to shift in a big way! The question is—what's next? Which leads to more questions: What am I aspiring to at this stage in my life? What is important for me to do now? What kind of legacy do I want to leave? And these questions lead us to re-vision or re-see the way we want to spend the next chapter(s) of our lives.

Here are my main takeaways from the research I performed for this workbook:

- Many soon-to-be and newly retired people want to continue working on some level. They want to be what I often call "retired-ish," whether working on a volunteer basis or not, once they've left their main chapter of work life. That can range from periodic to seasonal to contract to part- or even full-time work. People in their 50s and beyond are also taking on more full- or part-time entrepreneurial careers; one study shows a rising proportion of self-employment among people 60+ compared to their younger counterparts.[9] This indicates a thirst not only for working on some level after retirement, but for working in a more self-driven way. Yet, according to a recent *Wall Street Journal* article, while "more people over 60 plan to continue working in the future ... no clear roadmap exists for how to do it."[10]

- Today's retirees are healthier and increasingly active. People are living longer than ever on a global basis, and retirees are engaging in a variety of sports and social activities that seem to be promoting better health. One researcher from McMaster University, for example, points out that "the nature of aging itself (is) changing, as older adults (are) reaching a more advanced age in better condition than generations before them."[11]

- A sense of purpose is critical to staying healthy, physically and mentally. Studies have shown that older adults who feel they have purpose have a lower risk of chronic conditions and premature mortality, higher levels of physical activity, better sleep, and healthier measures of body mass,[12] in addition to better cognitive function and lower dementia risk.[13]

- People want engaging second (or third, fourth, fifth...) chapters aligned with who they see themselves becoming in the future.

Based on these insights, I began to realize that it was, indeed, both important and possible to transfer my expertise in vision from the business world to people who are on the brink of retirement—or those who have already made the leap. I decided to incorporate my research results, practical experience, and some real-life examples into a detailed workbook to help meet the need for a greater sense of connection, meaning, and enjoyment for those re-visioning retirement.

MY RE-VISIONING METHOD

I call the method I've developed to proactively move toward the reality of a satisfying retirement "FUN Re-Visioning" (you'll learn about what FUN means a little later!).

Think of vision as how your desired goals appear to you—like a cinematic preview of your future playing in your mind's eye. So re-visioning, at its core, is a process of rethinking what this best-case future could potentially look like for you. In doing so, you compare the goals and visions you had set for yourself based on your past values with those you aim for in the future, and you come up with a plan to layer them together and bridge the gaps in between. You can begin to view your future in a new light—one sometimes involving new or different focal points and aspirations.

I began by giving this personal re-visioning process a litmus test. I tested it out first on myself. And thanks to going through that process, I'm already seeing the benefits. I am prioritizing building my energy resources—physically, emotionally, and spiritually—in order to be better able to "give back" by providing a road map to other new and about-to-be retirees who are re-visioning their next chapter.

In order to create this workbook, I conducted research using both interviews and focus groups, which has been both fun and illuminating. I have also launched a new business to better work directly with new and about-to-be retirees; my work includes giving keynote speeches, continuing to write on the topic, and developing related courses. (But my vision isn't only about this workbook; I am also taking chess lessons with the grandmaster I followed for years on YouTube—and am finally able to give my husband a good game once in a while!)

My research included conversations with scores of people at various stages of the retiring process. Not unexpectedly, numerous people said they felt directionless and/or fearful of moving toward an undefined future. At the same time, I was inspired to see how many shared a desire to create deeper meaning in the period after their main work years. My conviction grew: I was not alone, as you are not alone. Many of us don't buy that retirement requires stopping work completely or ceasing to engage in meaningful activities. Retirement can mean *starting* anew ... whatever you set your sights on, whatever you envision.

THE INVITATION

You likely already have a lot figured out in life. But now, for this next phase of your life, you are keen to hone skills that will help bring it to a new level. FUN Re-Visioning is my solution for today's cohort of retirees. In this workbook, I offer practical skills, strategies, and knowledge to help you set a course toward a value-full and satisfying future.

As a recently retired professor and an international keynote speaker and author on the topic of the power of vision, I am an experienced voice on this subject. Incorporating some of the visioning tools I have spent three decades developing for organizations and entrepreneurs, this workbook can help retirees or soon-to-be retirees create meaningful goals that fit their personal vision and values. My intention with this workbook is to help close the gap between the desire *for* and the reality *of* a happier and more fulfilling retirement. I invite you to dive in!

The Opportunity

The opportunity, enabled through vision-setting, is for you to work toward long-term aspirational goals in a fun and engaging way and, possibly, even make a difference in the world.

As you know, though, dedicating yourself to such a process takes commitment and sometimes even some risk. Just like anything you do that's worthwhile, this workbook asks you to commit your time, energy, and focus. Visioning can also help you realize goals, though I obviously can't make any guarantees. The possibility of achieving specific outcomes is too riddled with changing circumstances to make such predictions. That said, I know that the re-visioning process can be a valuable tool on many levels; most importantly, going through it can help you learn about yourself and open up to the world in new ways.

We will also look at the positives associated with letting go of our attachments to outcomes and, instead, focusing on the journey—the subtle art of "becoming" who we desire and are inspired to be. Creating a vision and moving toward it can be valuable in and of itself. So I am cheering you on and encouraging you to have fun while you move through your own personal journey, and to embrace whatever way it might unfold!

I hope this *Re-Visioning Retirement* workbook inspires you and provides creative and practical guidance for developing a vision for the next phase of your life, whether it be a full-time next career, part-time work, or pursuing your passions and aspirations.

Throughout this workbook, we're going to explore how crafting and nurturing your vision has the potential to impact your personal life. This could range from enhancing your well-being to indulging in activities that light your soul on fire.

Your vision isn't just a wish list. It's a North Star for creating a road map to a more fulfilling and purposeful existence.

Let's get started!

THE POWER OF VISION

AT THIS POINT, AFTER READING THE INTRODUCTION and a little about re-visioning, you are probably saying, "Okay, Susan. Just what, exactly, is vision—and re-visioning? And why are they important for me to understand and apply to my future?"

To answer these questions, the best place to begin is by giving you a fuller understanding of what vision is, its main aspects, and why it's important. Then we can move on to the re-visioning process and how it can apply to you. Finally, I provide a road map for what I call FUN Re-Visioning, involving three pillars—Foundations, Uncovering, Nurturing—and a Prep Exercise to get you started. In later chapters, we'll dive into the FUN Re-Visioning pillars in detail with more exercises.

WHAT IS VISION?

Let's start with a definition.

In a nutshell, **a vision is simply a clear and specific mental image of one or more future goals that you want to achieve because they are important and inspiring to you.**

In other words, vision is how your desired goals appear to you in your mind's eye—it's the world you want to see!

Regardless of the particular goals involved, vision can always be described in four main ways: by its **form** (the who, what, when), **scope** (how big the vision is), **clarity** (how well it is defined), and **magnetism** (your passion for the goal).

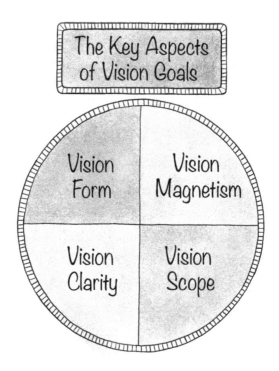

VISION FORM

The **form of the vision** is what the potential future goal actually looks like and what it represents to the visioner. It tends to involve three main aspects:

- **Who** is involved
- **What** is involved
- **When** it will happen (note that sometimes the timing doesn't matter or sometimes it's an "ongoing thing")

EXAMPLE 1: Oprah Winfrey, founder of OWN, the Oprah Winfrey Network, set out her vision this way: "To be a teacher. And to be known for inspiring my students to be more than they thought they could."[14] In this case, the **who** is both Oprah and those she wishes to inspire, the **what** is being a teacher, and the **when** is ongoing.

Oprah conveyed her vision by means of a vision statement, an invaluable tool for articulating the direction you want to follow and the way in which it appears in your mind's eye.

EXAMPLE 2: Rosalynn Carter, former First Lady of the United States, showed a clear vision to care for others by founding the Institute for Caregivers in 1987. Here, the **who** is caregivers and those whom they help, the **what** is care for others, and the **when** is ongoing.

EXAMPLE 3: Frederick W. Smith, founder of FedEx in the 1970s, had a business vision to offer mail and package delivery for businesses (the **who**), to provide overnight service (the **when**), and to use a "Super Hub" (the **what**), the first of which was located in Memphis, Tennessee.[15]

The form of the envisioned goal can be the part that takes the most time and reflection. As such, much of this workbook focuses on activities meant to help you come to a meaningful goal that can be grown, re-visioned, and clarified over time, as best suits your needs.

VISION SCOPE

The **scope** of the vision relates to its size, its potential for impact based on how many people it involves, and the length of the time frames involved. The scope may also include the number of elements making up the vision, and the number of connections between those elements.

EXAMPLE: Habitat for Humanity's vision is to create "a world where everyone has a decent place to live."[16] In this case, the magnitude is global, with a huge potential social impact and a long-term time frame. Jonathan Reckford, as of this writing in 2025, continues to pursue this vision, originally set forth in 1976.

Determining the scope of a goal clarifies whether moving toward the goal is something you want to do for yourself, for others in your life, or more broadly for an impact on different levels of society (community, city/town, country, the world, etc.). It sometimes also relates to whether you envision a financial aspect to the goal or not. The scope can start small and grow over time, or sometimes vice versa, if you decide to bite off a smaller piece of your original vision to concentrate on. Longer-term vision tends to have broader potential for impact, either because you have more time to enact the vision, because more people are involved, and/or because you have more shorter-term goals affiliated with it.

VISION CLARITY

A vision with good **clarity** has its form and scope expressed in a well-articulated way. Clarity is a powerful tool. When a vision is clear, it enables building a more well-defined and efficient plan toward its achievement. For example, in the business world, research shows that a clear vision can improve an organization's relations with its employees and customers, thereby improving success with meeting targets. On the other hand, organizations that fail to provide clarity to their employees on their roles and what they are working to achieve are often not successful.

Similarly, for your purposes, the clearer and more precise your vision, the more quickly you can see how to build a path toward your goal and improve chances of success in achieving it.

How do you achieve clarity? You need to make your vision tangible and specific. You do this by creating vivid portrayals—using both descriptions and images—outlining the building blocks of your vision's form. Say what the vision is, who will do it, and when. Then explain how you will achieve this vision, with a specific action plan.

Example: Diana Nyad had the incredible vision to swim from Cuba to Key West after turning 60.[17] She achieved success at age 64 on her fifth attempt! This is a great example of a long-term vision realized through incredible effort and by defining many specific shorter-term goals to help clarify what was necessary to get there.

Vision Magnetism

Whatever your vision's goal, scope, or level of clarity, the hallmark of vision is the passion dedicated to the idea of its achievement. It's what distinguishes between an intention to run a couple of times a week on the treadmill because it's recommended by the doctor, and the vision to set a personal best time in a 5K race. Passion is crucial. It helps to overcome inertia, can speed up the goal attainment process, and helps to attract others to your idea. A magnetic goal you are passionate about, therefore, helps not only to create a compelling vision but also to achieve it. When thinking about how passionate you are about a goal, remember the advice of organizing expert Marie Kondo: "Ask yourself if it sparks joy."[18] If it doesn't, let it go!

So, as you move through this workbook and beyond, continue to think about your vision goal. Are you passionate enough about it to dedicate yourself to achieving the goal? Are your sights set in a way that motivates you? Can it improve your life, and perhaps the lives of others? According to Jackie Roberge, a long-time friend and purpose coach, "We all have a deep desire to make a meaningful contribution in life. Living a purposeful life leads to true and lasting fulfilment and flow in everyday life." She also notes that "following your passion often leads you to your purpose," which can in turn help you to live "at a much more meaningful level."[19]

EXAMPLE: Walt Disney's historic corporate vision—"Make people happy"[20]—was representative of the passions of the founder. The company has continuously strived to make its original vision a mission through the realization of a multitude of projects, bringing happiness to people around the world for over a century.

WHY IS VISION IMPORTANT?

There is a story that you may have heard about the three bricklayers. When asked what they were working on, they responded in turn:

"Laying bricks."
"Building a wall."
"Erecting a great cathedral!"

The first bricklayer was simply working on a task. The second was thinking a little bigger, but he was still focused on a task. The third bricklayer, on the other hand, was propelled by a great vision, building a cathedral. Imagine how much more passionate he was while laying the bricks! Can you see how the scope of the vision has the ability to transform a daily task?

A clear and compelling vision with a potentially impactful scope, as we see with the example above, can help keep your goals aligned with your values and therefore, usually, offer a goal you are passionate about.

Visions can also be short and specific, or longer term and multifaceted. A longer-term vision can be focussed on an achievable goal based on your current motivations and resources. But longer-term visions can also represent what Jim Collins and Jerry Porras, authors of *Built to Last*,[21] call "big, hairy, audacious goals."[22] This type of goal is what I would call "aspirational," based on values you aspire to. They're not necessarily offering a final destination, but rather a general direction to follow. And, often, they may feel just a little out of reach. You may remember Michelangelo's famous painting from the Sistine Chapel, *The Creation of Adam*, of "man" reaching out to try to touch God's finger—almost, but not quite. A long-term vision can sometimes feel a little like that.

So, while some visions (particularly shorter-term visions) may result in reachable final achievements, others may provide a compass guiding the direction of your activities and aspirations throughout your life, and potentially beyond (as in the case of Walt Disney).

Long-Term Vision: The First Moon Landing

A well-known example of a successfully executed long-term vision is US president John F. Kennedy's goal, set out for NASA in 1961, to land a man on the moon before the end of the 1960s (note that the **who, what,** and **when** of the goal were clearly stated in the vision). When Kennedy announced this decade-long dream, engineers from NASA would have understood that they had to start with some more concrete, shorter-term, vision-driven goals to make it happen. For example, training pilots to become astronauts, building a lunar landing module and rocket ship became tangible steps in realizing the more grandiose, longer-term vision of landing on the moon.

So you can see that sometimes you may need to enact shorter-term visions over an extended period of time while you develop the skills and assemble the resources required to accomplish the broader, longer-term vision.

SHORT-TERM VISION:
BOB PROCTOR AND HIS YO-YO

As explained in the previous example, shorter-term visions can serve as stepping stones for achieving longer-term visions. But sometimes, they involve self-directed goals that can provide satisfaction in their own right. Shorter-term visions also offer the opportunity to try out and learn about new things so that you can connect with yourself on a meaningful level. For example, many competitive sports use short-term visioning to help narrow the gap between theory and practice and can provide athletes with manageable goals. Yoga, meditation, and certain psychological practices likewise use visioning techniques to enable people to achieve focus, clarity, insight, and self-awareness.

One individual who set a clear and passionate personal vision, achievable in the short term, was the legendary Canadian self-help author and motivational speaker Bob Proctor.

Bob Proctor used to start some of his seminars with a fantastic yo-yo show. During a seminar I attended, he said he hadn't become so skilled simply by focusing on the techniques of how to become a yo-yo whiz; that was a by-product. Rather, the goal of his vision was very clear: to win a yo-yo competition because he was passionately driven to earn the championship jacket that went with the win. In other words, he developed his yo-yo skills as a means to an end. And, if I remember correctly, he brought that decades-old jacket out on stage and modelled it for us while performing some dazzling yo-yo tricks and telling his story about how he had won it.

So, you see, Bob Proctor had been passionate about a clear goal—winning the championship jacket in the annual competition—and he needed three key things to bring clarity to that goal: the **who** (him), the **what** (the jacket), and the **when** (that year). A plan for accomplishing what he had set out to do in his mind—honing the skills to win the competition—came only after he had set his vision. In other words, the planning piece came after the vision-setting piece.

Clearly, Bob Proctor and his yo-yo, as an example of vision-setting and its benefits, have stuck with me; it's been at least 30 years since I attended that seminar. And his vision evolution—from becoming a great yo-yo player in his younger years to later becoming a wonderful motivational speaker—was also a lesson about evolving aspirations that I took to heart as my own visions shifted over the years.

Thinking about President Kennedy's long-term moon-landing vision, which became a reality over the better part of a decade, and Bob Proctor's shorter-term championship yo-yo jacket vision motivated me to learn more about vision through my research and personal vision-setting over the years.

> ### My Personal Visioning Story
>
> After kicking off my career with a biology degree in hand and a job in the field, I quickly became inspired by some of the visionaries I worked with. Around that same time, I also started listening to speakers like Bob Proctor and Jim Rohn and became enthralled by the topic of vision, eventually studying it and making it the focus of my PhD. In other words, I came up with a vision for the direction of my life.
>
> *Continued...*

SUSAN REID

> But, despite my now long-standing interest in vision, I seem to have a knack for jumping into major life-changing events with both feet and no plan, based largely on intuition and gut feel—and then figuring out the vision to try to make it successful afterwards! But what I've realized is that how you arrive at your vision may not be as important as the act of creating the vision itself—whether it comes from starting with a gut feeling first, or intentionally looking to switch things up. Either way, you can be proactive in bringing things to fruition by constructing a vision statement to further crystallize how to move forward with planning and enacting that vision.
>
> Case in point. Shortly after my husband and I were married, over 30 years ago, we bought a vintage farmhouse (circa 1859) in Frelighsburg, Quebec. We did that before really considering what we were going to do with the 430-acre apple orchard we'd acquired along with the house. Long story short: it became pretty apparent that we were going to need a plan for all those apples—and quickly. Most people said "cut down the trees" or "start up a Christmas tree farm"...
>
> We did neither, instead quickly coming up with a vision and accompanying vision statement to be the "#1

Continued...

> apple ice cider producer in the world," which we followed through on (and have since sold)!
>
> That may seem straightforward, but having that vision helped us chart a path forward from the unknown to success. Proof positive that having a vision (and creating a vision statement to give it legs!) can sometimes be the difference between achieving big goals and just getting through the tasks of the day.

WHY IS RE-VISIONING RETIREMENT IMPORTANT?

If you are like me, and you've just retired or you are contemplating retirement, creating a clear and compelling vision of your future can propel you into a fun and fulfilling next chapter of life. Re-visioning offers many advantages to the new retiree. It gives us the chance to see our future through a new lens, one which can be illuminating and energizing. For those of us at a certain age, it can also be a way to revitalize ourselves and fend off some of the "internalized ageism" that hinders some older people in our society.[23] Indeed, based on my research, one of the greatest concerns with retirement is the fear of the loss of one's importance or ability to be of use to society—this is what one of my friends calls her fear of the "invisibility cloak."[24]

Having a strong vision of what we want to do in the future offers a useful antidote to that problem. It can shine a guiding light into the murky world of life after a career.

For those of us wishing to continue working on some level, re-visioning retirement can help us figure out what we truly want to focus our work-related efforts on at this stage, and how. Obviously, pervasive expertise gaps in the workforce exist owing to the departure of so many experienced workers, particularly during the "Big Quit." The loss of senior-level expertise is and will increasingly become a loss for society unless some of it can be attracted back to the table. But doing so needs to address many retirees' desire to be more autonomous (i.e., free from some or all organizational constraints) and to address the need for incorporating more personal vision into the equation.

This is a generation of young retirees looking for ways to be re-engaged and re-empowered. At a time when society is looking for good role models and leadership, we can be part of the solution. We can lean back into being involved in our communities in ways that are aligned with our values and who we want to be, and how.

My Personal Re-Visioning Story

I had always expected that my work with vision that began during my PhD would be applied to helping businesses and entrepreneurs to attain their goals. But, when I retired from the university and we sold our family business and orchard, some of my underlying values and motivators started to shift. This, in turn, changed how I viewed my future and underpinned what became my new long-term vision involving helping other people with their own personal visioning.

I became increasingly interested in the act and process of re-visioning, not only for businesses, as I had originally focused on, but also for individuals—particularly those people at a crossroads in their lives, such as those transitioning through retirement. So the "what" of my long-term vision did not change; however, in order to fulfill it and bring it to more people, a shift was required in terms of my vision's scope and in the "who" I was working with. As I became more interested in giving back and the legacy I wanted to create, I realized the importance of focusing on "retired-ish" individuals, particularly retirees or semi-retirees who were looking to up their personal game.

Creating a Vision—and Then Changing It

As I've highlighted in my personal visioning and re-visioning stories, when it comes to a personal vision, new opportunities of interest and/or challenging circumstances may arise to change things over time. Your own internal desires and values may also start to shift, sometimes on their own or sometimes in combination with external circumstances, bringing about the need or desire for change. These forces can stimulate rethinking, re-visiting, and, in a more directed or conscious way, re-visioning your future! Revising your original vision is the essence of re-visioning.

Retirement offers a ground-shaking change paired with a myriad of new opportunities and perhaps the desire to rethink your values. In my case, for example, I had always been driven by a strong need for achievement. Having very achievement-oriented goals seemed normal for the earlier stages of life; but at the dawn of my retirement, I realized that a pure achievement orientation wasn't really doing it for me anymore (although, of course, it would always probably play some role in my underlying motivation set!).

Does Everyone Need to Re-Vision Retirement?

I was thrown a great question in a seminar I gave recently: "Isn't it okay to live day to day and just get out of each one what it has to offer?" To which I responded that if your vision is to live spontaneously—and you are passionate about it—that's an amazing vision! Very *The Power of Now*.[25] The ability to do so is certainly a high-level aspiration for many people.

Another question that comes up often is whether it's possible and/or necessary to create a vision for your retirement ... and how doing so might offer the potential to create new opportunities, new possibilities, and sometimes even new careers. In other words, you may be asking yourself whether it's possible to create a vision that is both viable and meaningful for you. Or put another way: Can I do it? And is it important for me to do it?

For me, of course, the answer on both counts is a wholehearted *yes*. First, you can try it: This book offers you a process to help you get there. Second, creating a vision can be a game-changer. I find that having a clear vision for the future makes the difference between sleepwalking through the rest of my life and living life to its fullest. To my mind, having a vision is not a luxury, given its role in helping us connect with our aspirations, consciousness, and identity, as well as with society. And for those of you who have held a vision during the first chapter(s) of your work life, and have been reasonably comfortable with it, you may want to challenge yourself to think about how you might want to re-vision and re-engage moving into the future.

We all intuitively understand that we can build our own experience in life, in conjunction with various internal and external factors and circumstances we can't always control. Visioning and re-visioning let you determine how that co-created experience might look. This workbook is designed to help you with that process.

The Elephant in the Room

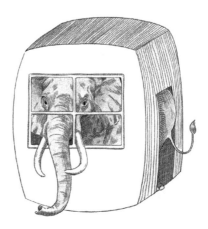

One common, often unfortunate, element of circumstance is that darn financial piece. In one of the surveys I conducted, I asked, "Do you already have a vision for your retirement from your current job?" Most people said they did not have a vision yet. They often had ideas for activities they might do, but a common concern, in some form or other, was that they were still figuring out the financial piece of the puzzle. I gave a webinar recently for hundreds of viewers and people were able to send me their questions in advance. The number-one question had to do with exactly this.

Finances are an important consideration for most people re-visioning retirement. Sometimes it means needing to work for longer than you would like. Sometimes it requires building an exit strategy from your current organization or self-employment situation. Sometimes it means letting go of some things, even what you might regard as comfortable financial security, to move in a new direction. While these may seem like hurdles, it is possible to treat them as shorter-term goals necessary for achieving your longer-term vision. In other words, it may mean that achieving adequate financial security becomes a key component of your re-visioning activities or that obtaining financial backing needs to be worked into the plan to achieve the main goal of the vision itself. You may ultimately decide that continuing to work part time offers the kind of balance you are seeking between fulfillment and financial security. These situations offer good examples of ways to develop shorter-term, vision-driven financial goals to support your aspirations moving forward!

Of course, there can be other barriers besides finances, such as health, education, and physical location. While these certainly cannot be dismissed, for many in such circumstances a vision can still be in one's mind and a tentative plan made to achieve it. Remember the movie *The Shawshank Redemption*, where the main character, jailed for almost 20 years of his life, finally achieves his vision to live in Zihuatanejo!

By definition, a long-term vision should always feel and be at least a little out of reach. The how-to behind big, lofty aspirational goals may not be immediately apparent, and that's why the shorter-term visions, the stepping stones that move you toward your longer-term visions, are so important. In chess, such shorter-term ideas and strategies are called "discovery moves." The idea is that you can't realize the next steps until you take the first steps, and then the next steps will naturally become more clear.

Mindset and Letting Go of Outcomes

Making active decisions with vision-setting and trying to follow through on them requires a certain mindset, one open to learning and change, while being true to your values. It also means being ready to reroute your path when circumstances or outcomes don't match your needs or expectations.

This open mindset is crucial at every step of this journey—from creating a vision to re-visioning as you move along your path. We'll talk about this more in Exercise 8.

One part of mindset is how attached we are to results. Does visioning need to lead to good outcomes for it to be worthwhile?

As guru Michael Singer explains in *The Surrender Experiment,* it was only once he allowed himself to surrender to what life presented that he began to understand what he calls his "simple formula for success: Do whatever is put in front of you with all your heart and soul without regard for personal results."[26]

When it comes to visions, the real success is experiencing the journey to its fullest. As one of my teachers, a spiritual guide, taught me, in your mind you get to choose your path and the experience you want to direct yourself along, even if the end goal is not where you ultimately end up. So outcomes ultimately may take a back seat to how you feel in the process of creating and trying to enact visions—whether you do or don't achieve them!

THE FUN RE-VISIONING PROCESS:
Foundations, Uncovering, Nurturing

So how might you create a vision for your retirement? By using this workbook to get inspired, get dreaming, and, at the end, get to a clear vision created by you, for you. The workbook I've developed guides you—exercise by exercise—through FUN Re-Visioning, my take on an inspirational path to help lead you to your vision.

FUN Re-Visioning is based on three pillars:

Foundations
- Understanding your authentic self

Uncovering
- Discovering your aspirational self

Nurturing
- Bringing your visionary self to life

Below is a visual representation of how the FUN Re-Visioning process unfolds. The three pillars work together leading to a vision. Continuing the re-visioning process over time can help direct you toward your North Star, or purpose. While the three pillars are set out along a timeline for simplicity in this workbook, they are, as indicated in the illustration, more accurately non-linear and overlapping. In fact, it may sometimes feel a little like the path is cyclical and gradually looping forward.

HOW TO USE THIS WORKBOOK: YOUR ROAD MAP TO FUN RE-VISIONING

Before starting your FUN Re-Visioning process, please read through the introduction and this chapter on the power of vision, including the Prep Exercise coming at the end of this chapter, to get you psyched up and ready for the work that follows.

To cover each pillar in enough detail, I suggest you move through this workbook allowing at least **one week for each pillar, with five exercises for you to do each week**.

I also urge you to **take a break of at least one week between the pillars**. Time is needed for the ideas and feelings that come up as you move through the process to blend, sift, and settle into a meaningful pattern. After Pillar 1, take a break for personal reflection and journalling. I've included some prompts to guide this process. After Pillar 2, a guided exercise is provided for further reflection.

Used as described above, the workbook takes a minimum of five weeks to go through—but you can complete it at whatever pace feels right. There is no right or wrong way, except that **I recommend that you do the exercises in order, as they've been designed accordingly.** Most of the exercises should take around 10 to 15 minutes, although a few might take a little longer. And a couple may involve a few days or more, allowing time to ponder before moving further through the workbook.

I suggest that you use a notebook to keep all your responses, notes, visuals, and ideas in one place. Your notebook will offer a unique and valuable record of your thoughts and emotions at this time in your life, a record you may refer to often.

I get it! Life's busy! But guess what? Carving out time to take on this process is not only for learning more about where you stand in terms of meeting your current goals. It's also an investment in your future self. Just as you wouldn't miss important obligations with work or family, I'm asking you to commit to yourself by spending some time on this journey. Consider it a rendezvous with your aspirations, and let the magic unfold!

Six Tips for a Great Experience

1. **Get in the "zone" before beginning each exercise.** Set yourself up by doing what works for you. This could involve clearing your space, blocking distractions, meditating, going for a walk, or taking a few deep breaths to get centred and ready to participate freely, fully, and openly.

2. **Be attentive to your feelings and reactions.** Sometimes when you start, you may feel tired, challenged, or not ready to proceed during an exercise. You will have moments of feeling like "Yes, this is me, this is what I want" and moments of sheer frustration when you feel blocked or perhaps skeptical of proceeding. Sometimes it flows; sometimes it doesn't—just like when I get writer's block. This is completely normal. If you need to take a break and come back later—even much later—no worries! Do it at your pace and in whatever way works best for you. Sometimes the inspiration will come to you right away in a kind of "aha" moment (like Archimedes and his "eureka moment" when he discovered the law of buoyancy while in the bath,

after pondering it for quite some time)[27] and sometimes—crickets. If so, just take a break. Doing something else is often the best way to let things brew for a bit and then percolate to the surface when they are good and ready.

3. **Be prepared to change your mind along the way.** Some questions will call for quicker answers and others require more contemplation. This may sometimes lead to changing your perspective and/or changing your mind altogether about the direction you are moving in. Many participants in my focus groups expressed that this happened to them—so it's completely normal! If this happens, I suggest you take a break (see previous point), and also, try to remain open—with both your mind and your heart.

    I also recommend that you revisit the themes you will be identifying in the Prep Exercise (coming up next!) after each pillar you work through. Please note that these areas of personal development, which you identify to focus on at the outset, may or may not relate to your developing vision. If you are moving forward in an unexpected way from what you had identified in the Prep Exercise, this is not unusual. The workbook focuses on opening up to new possibilities and, therefore, to goals or ideals you might not have considered relevant, achievable, or even desirable in the past.

    It's easy to stay in the comfort zone, but personal growth sometimes comes from pushing outside the edges into discomfort until those boundaries start to feel comfortable. Then, if it makes sense and feels right, keep on going.

Journalling during your break weeks will help you see where there might be relationships and overlap between your initial thoughts and personal development themes (Prep Exercise coming up) and new ideas that surface during the main workbook exercises. You will also see whether things come up during the process that change where you want to put emphasis with your aspirations for this period in your life. These notes will help you to explore your various values and goals and how the re-visioning process may bring up new ideas for you to bring into your awareness and heart.

4. **Trust in your own path.** In our society we've been taught to compare ourselves with others in order to measure success. Some people may wonder if the vision they are working toward is important enough or worthwhile. There is no metric by which to compare yourself with others on this. The only person who can tell you about whether your vision is worthwhile is you!

5. **Know that fears are normal when challenging yourself.** Many people I have worked with say that once they start putting things in writing as they move through the exercises, they start feeling fears regarding the vision they are working toward. This is normal because "the act of writing things down makes things more concrete and the ego can get defensive, because its role is to keep us safe."[28] This is something to be attuned to while completing all the exercises in the workbook. If you are successful in

creating a vision and getting clear on it, what might that bring up for you? It could bring up fears around success, for example, as it did for me in writing this workbook: "Will the workbook live up to everyone's expectations?" Or you might be concerned that "I will be too busy and I don't want that at this stage in my life," or "Maybe this vision is not the right one."

It's entirely normal to ask such questions and voice such fears—I have asked them of myself, many times! But the fact that I was passionate about my vision and my desire to work with retirees helped me understand that I needed to move past my fears. Also, as I did, you may need to set up some boundaries in terms of time commitments and expectations to help minimize those concerns. The beauty of re-visioning is that it is an ongoing process and one we can adapt and clarify as we desire over time.

6. **Give yourself a pat on the back (figuratively and/or literally) after every single exercise you complete.** When I used to run a 5K at our orchard, there was a yield sign by the roadside I would high-five every time I finished that run—it was a way of patting myself on the back, letting myself know that I'd achieved my mini-goal, and reminding myself that it was helping me build toward my bigger, longer-term vision of running a marathon. A little reward after completing each exercise and section will increase your enjoyment and acknowledge your commitment as you move through this process.

▬ TRY THIS PREP EXERCISE ▬

Let's get your feet wet by delving into a high-level visioning exercise to immediately give you a sense of where we'll be heading throughout the rest of this workbook. Going through this exercise will help you see why creating a vision for yourself can be a game-changer.

I suggest that you do this Prep Exercise before beginning the FUN Re-Visioning process and perhaps circle back to your responses to this exercise later in the process or once you have completed the workbook. It will be interesting to see how you relate to what you wrote here at the beginning. Then allow yourself some time for reflection and continue to tweak and re-vision as you desire.

Let's begin by taking a closer look at some potential areas you may wish to focus your attention on while participating in this re-visioning process!

➤ Think about three broad personal development themes that immediately come to mind.

Get into the zone, relax, then ask yourself: "What three areas of personal development are important for me?" Write down what comes up first—without judgment. Some examples might be health, family, relationships, pursuing personal activities, developing a business idea, spiritual growth. Make sure to keep these areas broad and only write down the theme. Your brain will naturally want to start a more specific goal-setting process right away, but tell it to hold on—we'll get there!

▷ **Elaborate a little more by jotting down a phrase or sentence to develop each of the three themes you would like to explore more.**

These sentences will offer some very broad goals to consider developing and looking into further in the future. For example, if one of your personal development themes is health, a broad elaboration might be something like "I want to get a better handle on my current health situation."

▷ **Dive deeper and explain why each of these matters to you right now.**

Again, remember—no specific goal-setting yet. Just write down a little about your "why"[29] behind each theme. For example, with the health theme, your answer to the "why" question might be: "After years at a desk job, I feel that my physical stamina—to stand, walk, lift, and so on—are not what they used to be, and this concerns me."

To reiterate, in these reflections, you don't need to detail specific goals that might be attached to the themes you have listed. You just need to think about what themes are of interest, potential broad goals that might be attached to them, and why they feel important to you at this time.

Closing Thoughts

Re-visioning your future is a remarkable opportunity. Allowing yourself to connect with areas that you know and feel you want to work on acts as a key to unlock a realm you may not have experienced to the extent you desire. So write down your dreams, prioritize them, and let the excitement build. Welcome to the start of this path!

PILLAR 1
Foundations (Week 1)

YOUR AUTHENTIC SELF

To understand your authentic self, you need to explore a simple question: What motivates you?

There are three key types of motivators providing a foundation for your actions and goals:

1. Your values
2. Your skills
3. Your passions

Getting to these foundations means peeling back the layers to uncover what inspires you at your core. These are the motivators that you typically lean toward when you set out to achieve any kind of activity or goal.

Pillar 1 sets the stage for re-visioning with five motivational awareness and development exercises. The first three exercises focus on bringing to light your values, your skills, and your passions. Exercises 4 and 5 expand on how these motivations knit together. They also provide food for thought as to how your core values might be further developed to provide energy for moving toward your future.

The aim of Pillar 1 is to create an outline to help understand what drives your authentic self—your core values, natural skills, and passions that have operated strongly in your past and present, and that will serve you as you explore your future. Think of your current motivations as your home base from which you hope to set up outposts to explore the unknown. Getting to know your authentic self, and how you might potentially build on it, offers a starting place for your own unique re-visioning path and a set of ideas for strengthening and revitalizing the most important aspects of your foundational core.

EXERCISE 1
EMBRACE YOUR AUTHENTIC SELF: VALUES

Please note: Exercise 1 may take at least one hour to complete. It is one of the longer time investments of the workbook and will help set the important groundwork for moving forward with re-visioning.

What are we talking about when we use the word *values*? Values encompass your guiding beliefs and interests in life, and, as such, are the silent architects of your choices. Your values influence the directions you follow, your activities, your goals—and, as we will see in the following exercises, your visions. In other words, as noted by renowned social scientist and values expert Shalom Schwartz, values "motivate action."[30]

The three most commonly shared values globally, and noted consistently by researchers, are family, respect, and honesty. That said, there are many kinds of values. Some, for example, reflect personal values like curiosity, freedom, and compassion. Others relate more to interpersonal values like relationships, family, and social justice. But what's important for this vision exercise are the values that influence *your* actions and *your* behaviour.

This exercise has two parts. In Part A, you will begin by thinking about your core values—your typical go-tos. While people might identify with many values, most of us lean toward a few that consistently drive us. In Part B, you will explore some specific types of values particularly relevant to re-visioning.

PART A
VALUES THAT RESONATE WITH YOU TODAY

➤ **Quickly list up to 10 values that are important to you.**
Let your instincts guide you and write down the most important values for you (up to 10) that immediately come to mind. If you need some examples to kick-start the process, do a quick search online for "list of values."

➤ **Circle one or two that stand out as important value drivers for your current activities.**
If you'd like to dig deeper into this topic, I'd recommend taking a standardized test to assess your values further. A variety of tests are available online, offering comprehensive value inventories. Keep in mind, values are diverse, and different methodologies emphasize different aspects of a person's value system.

PART B
ACTIVATOR VALUES

Here we will look specifically at values related to embracing new opportunities and taking on new challenges. I call them *activator values*.

There are two kinds of activator values that may help you think more clearly about how to move the needle on activating and realizing your vision. The first kind, **psycho-social values**, reflect the ideals of individuals and affect their behaviour. The second kind, **altruistic-biospheric values**, advocate benefits for others and for the environment.

Published research shows that certain types of psycho-social values—learning goal orientation, self-efficacy, autonomy, and innovativeness (each explained below)—consistently help drive new goal-oriented and visionary activities forward. So, when we re-vision our lives, these values can be highly relevant for us to consider. Each of these four psycho-social values has a scale in the exercise below made up of questions relevant to visioning.

I'm also introducing altruistic-biospheric values into the mix of activator values. Social and environmental issues are two of the most profound topics facing society today, and similar to activating types of psycho-social values, altruistic-biospheric values can motivate people to take on new challenges. The inventory (comprising two scales) provided at the end of this exercise measures this inclination to take on challenges related to improving the welfare of others and the environment.

GENERAL INSTRUCTIONS

At the beginning of each scale is an explanation about what is being measured and how to complete the questions. There are no right or wrong answers here. Rather, your answers are meant to provide some insights about your inclination to take on new opportunities and challenges (as related to activator values), which may tend to direct how you interact with new ideas and situations. Again, there are no judgments here—the information is for your own insight, interpretation, and use, moving forward.

For simplicity, all tests use a seven-point scale.

▷ How to score each scale

1. Add up your ratings for all of the questions/items making up each scale.

2. Divide that total by the number of questions/items in the scale to come up with your average on each scale.

3. Record the scale title and your average in your notebook.

LEARNING GOAL ORIENTATION SCALE

"Learning Goal Orientation indicates one's general belief that abilities are malleable and can be developed, an incremental perspective on ability."[31]

On a scale from 1 to 7, score yourself on each of the following eight Learning Goal Orientation Scale statements.[32]

Definitely Not		Definitely Yes
Strongly DISAGREE	Neutral	Strongly AGREE
1 · · · 2 · · · 3	· · · 4 · · · 5	· · · 6 · · · 7

1. The opportunity to do challenging work is important to me.
2. When I fail to complete a difficult task, I plan to try harder the next time I work on it.
3. I prefer to work on tasks that force me to learn new things.
4. The opportunity to learn new things is important to me.
5. I do my best when I'm working on a fairly difficult task.
6. I try hard to improve on my past performance.
7. The opportunity to extend the range of my abilities is important to me.
8. When I have difficulty solving a problem, I enjoy trying different approaches to see which one will work.

To get your Learning Goal Orientation average, total your ratings and divide by 8.

GENERALIZED SELF-EFFICACY SCALE

"Self-efficacy" is a belief about how well we think we can accomplish goals and come up with solutions to problems.[33] In other words, it is an indication of self-confidence.

On a scale from 1 to 7, score yourself on each of the following eight Generalized Self-Efficacy Scale statements.[34]

Definitely Not		Definitely Yes
Strongly DISAGREE	Neutral	Strongly AGREE
1 . . . . 2 . . . . 3 . . . . 4 . . . . 5 . . . . 6 7		

1. I will be able to achieve most of the goals that I have set for myself.
2. When facing difficult tasks, I am certain that I will accomplish them.
3. In general, I think that I can obtain outcomes that are important to me.
4. I believe I can succeed at most any endeavor to which I set my mind.
5. I will be able to successfully overcome many challenges.
6. I am confident that I can perform effectively on many different tasks.
7. Compared to other people, I can do most tasks very well.
8. Even when things are tough, I can perform quite well.

To get your Self-Efficacy average, total your ratings and divide by 8.

AUTONOMY SCALE

"Autonomy" can be described as one's investment in persevering and increasing independence, mobility, and personal rights. It reflects the ability and proclivity to make informed, yet self-governed, decisions.[35]

On a scale from 1 to 7, score yourself on each of the following eight Autonomy (Independent Goal Attainment) Scale statements.[36]

Definitely Not		Definitely Yes
Strongly DISAGREE	Neutral	Strongly AGREE
1 · · · 2 · · · 3 · · ·	4 · · · ·	5 · · · 6 · · · 7

1. If a goal is important to me, I will pursue it even if it may make other people uncomfortable.

2. The possibility of being rejected by others for standing up for my rights would not stop me.

3. I set my own standards and goals for myself rather than accepting those of other people.

4. If I think I am right about something, I feel comfortable expressing myself even if others don't like it.

5. It is more important to meet your own objectives on a task than to meet another person's objective.

6. When I achieve a goal, I get more satisfaction from reaching the goal than from any praise I might get.

7. It is more important that I know I've done a good job than having others know it.

8. I enjoy accomplishing things more than being given credit for them.

To get your Autonomy average, total your ratings and divide by 8.

INDIVIDUAL INNOVATIVENESS SCALE

"Innovativeness" refers to a "willingness to change"[37] as well as a "willingness to adopt new information and ideas and act on them."[38] Some researchers even say it is about willingness to engage in something difficult. It's about creativity, imagination, and originality.

The Innovativeness Scale involves 10 items/statements.[39] On a scale from 1 to 7, score yourself on the first of the statements.

Note: The scale is reversed after the first question.

Definitely Not Strongly DISAGREE	Neutral	Definitely Yes Strongly AGREE
1 · · · 2 · · · 3 · · ·	4 · · ·	5 · · · 6 · · · 7

1. I find it stimulating to be original in my thinking and behavior.

On a scale from 7 to 1, score yourself on each of the remaining nine Innovativeness Scale items/statements.

Definitely Not		Definitely Yes
Strongly DISAGREE	Neutral	Strongly AGREE
7 · · · · · 6 · · · · · 5 · · · · · 4 · · · · · 3 · · · · · 2 · · · · · 1		

2. I am generally cautious about accepting new ideas.
3. I rarely trust new ideas until I can see whether the vast majority of people around me accept them.
4. I am aware that I am usually one of the last people in my group to accept something new.
5. I am reluctant about adopting new ways of doing things until I see them working for people around me.
6. I tend to feel that the old way of living and doing things is the best way.
7. I am challenged by ambiguities and unsolved problems.
8. I must see other people using new innovations before I will consider them.
9. I am suspicious of new inventions and new ways of thinking.
10. I often find myself skeptical of new ideas.

To get your Innovativeness average, total your ratings and divide by 10.

ALTRUISTIC-BIOSPHERIC INVENTORY

In decision-making or goal-setting situations, altruistic values indicate the inclination to advocate benefits on behalf of others; biospheric values indicate a desire to include the environment as a key consideration. Taken together, they offer a measure of valuing humanitarian efforts in combination with pro-environmentalism.

On a scale from 1 to 7, score yourself on each of the following nine Altruistic-Biospheric Inventory statements.[40]

Definitely Not		Definitely Yes
Strongly DISAGREE	Neutral	Strongly AGREE
1 · · · 2 · · · 3 · · ·	4 · · ·	5 · · · 6 · · · 7

Altruistic Items

1. It is important that every person has equal opportunities.

2. It is important to take care of those who are worse off.

3. It is important that every person is treated justly.

4. It is important that there is no war or conflict.

5. It is important to be helpful to others.

Biospheric Items

1. It is important to prevent environmental pollution.

2. It is important to protect the environment.

3. It is important to respect nature.

4. It is important to be in unity with nature.

To get your Altruistic and Biospheric average, total your ratings for all nine questions and divide by 9. Alternatively, if you are interested in your results for each category, total your Altruistic ratings and divide by 5, and total your Biospheric ratings and divide by 4.

What Can This Exercise Tell You About Yourself?

You have calculated an average value for each scale. For example, for Learning Goal Orientation (which has a total of eight questions), if your answers were 6, 5, 7, 6, 7, 6, 5, 5, your total would be 47. Divide this by 8 (the number of questions), and your average would be 5.875. Since 4 is neutral with the scales used, a score of 5–7 indicates that the learning goal factor may play a role for you in terms of how you tend to embrace working toward goals and opportunities/challenges. Please note that, while each scale is distinct from the others, some may be correlated on a low level. So you may have similar scores for some factors.

A comparison of your averages across the five inventories offers some food for thought. Look at your average for each inventory to get a general sense of the importance of each activator value in your motivation set as it pertains to goals and exposure to new ideas, opportunities, or challenges. Your scores may suggest some ideas for where you tend to put emphasis for goal attainment and decision-making when confronted with such new information. Your answers may also help you focus in the next exercises on ways to start your visioning activities that are aligned with your primary activator values.

Again, there are no right or wrong answers. Keep in mind that one person's 5 may be a 6 for another. There are no absolutes with these types of measures. Your answers give you subjective scores, relevant only for you, and point you toward understanding your own "secret sauce" combination of activator values. Think of this as a key for helping you unlock new situations. Some people may use a broad approach drawing on all of these factors; others may tend to rely more on some factors than others.

How Can You Apply What You've Learned Here?

The aim of this exercise is to give you an idea of which values tend to drive your existing behaviour as it relates to being presented with new situations. As we'll see, this is a crucial foundation for your journey to create a new vision for yourself. Why? Because vision needs to be aligned with how you operate—with the values driving your actions today. This alignment, if employed, can offer more ease and satisfaction throughout the visioning process.

You don't need to "do" anything specific with the numerical value averages you have noted down for the inventories. The goal is to use them as a tool for reflection and building self-awareness.

Closing Thoughts

Consider this saying that drives home the importance of values: "Your thoughts become your words, your words become your actions, your actions become your habits, your habits become your values, your values become your destiny."[41]

EXERCISE 2

EMBRACE YOUR AUTHENTIC SELF: SKILLS AND LEARNING STYLES

There are three parts to the following exercise:

1. Identifying skills that you're naturally good at and/or have honed and enjoy doing
2. Identifying your natural learning styles
3. Weaving the two together, by thinking about how awareness of this combination of skills and learning styles can help your re-visioning journey

YOUR NATURAL SKILLS

➢ **In your notebook, list the first three natural skills that immediately pop into your mind.**

1. _____
2. _____
3. _____

➢ **Jot down some further thoughts next to the three skills you've listed.**

- Are they hard skills (technical or manual skills)?
- Are they soft skills (people skills, communication, or creativity)?

- Perhaps a mix of both?
- Do you see using any or all of these skills as a focal point for moving forward in your visioning journey? In a support role? Do they intersect or are they distinct?
- Note these down.

YOUR NATURAL LEARNING STYLES

▷ **From the list below, choose the way that best captures how you prefer to process information.**

- Reading/Writing
- Physical/Kinesthetic
- Visual/Graphic representation
- Auditory

Free questionnaires are available online if you aren't sure which learning style/s you gravitate to.

▷ **List secondary learning styles you also gravitate toward.**

▷ **Note down the mode(s) of learning and representing information that feel most comfortable for you.**

For example: journalling, audio recording, drawing, videoing, building, vision boarding, or another form of personal expression you are drawn to. Write down your preferred modes along with a comment to yourself as to how they might support and enrich your visioning journey moving forward.

SKILLS + LEARNING STYLES

▷ **Give an example of how one of your natural skills intersects with one of your learning styles.**

▷ **Use this connection to show how it has helped or might help you to achieve a goal.**

Skill + Learning Style (Running + Visual)

I love and gravitate to distance running. I also have a preference for visual information. So, to assist with training for a marathon or half-marathon, I represent my running goals visually, showing weekly goals leading to the overall goal.

How Can You Apply What You've Learned Here?

During the goal-setting process for this workbook and moving forward, it is useful to consider your go-to modes for expressing your thoughts and desires and translating them into something more tangible. Doing so offers a natural call to action and a way to more easily understand and clarify early steps in moving toward your bigger goals. Thought capturing—in the most authentic and natural way for you—slows things down, allows a snapshot of where you are now, and bridges it to where you want to be and how you might get there.

Closing Thoughts

Bringing your skills and learning style(s) into your awareness helps you move along your path in a lighter, more engaging, and natural way. Your understanding of your authentic self is gaining depth now. Let's see it flourish!

EXERCISE 3
EMBRACE YOUR AUTHENTIC SELF: PASSIONS

We've talked about motivators based on values and skills. Here, we dive into a third motivator: your passions. "Passion" can be defined as "a strong feeling of enthusiasm or excitement for something or about doing something."[42] As mentioned previously, passion is what distinguishes having any old goal from having a vision.

This is the first—but not the last!—time I'll guide you to pause and breathe deeply before starting the exercise. This will calm you, get you into your own grounded rhythm and flow, and help you to connect with your intuition.

> **Close your eyes and take a few deep breaths.**

> **When you're ready, open your eyes.**

> **Write down whatever immediately pops into your head for each of the following prompts.**

1. List five topics, ideas, and activities that your best friend(s) would say you are most passionate about.

2. Prioritize the list, from 1 to 5 (highest to lowest), in terms of your own passion level for these activities. Is there anything else you would add to this list (perhaps a secret passion)?

3. Beside each of the five items, write down what makes you feel good about the idea or activity. For example, which of your underlying core values or natural skills are expressed through such activities? Some suggestions to get you thinking: guiding or helping others, leadership, giving back, creating a legacy, achieving, and so on.

It's okay if these things are already obvious to you. The key is to prioritize the ideas, clarify your thoughts about them, and gain a better understanding of the link between the "what" (ideas and activities you are passionate about) and the "why" (values and skills), in each case.

A Passion for Coaching

When I asked a friend how she got into personal coaching, she told me: "One of my passions is mentoring others (priority #1). The 'why' behind this passion is tied to my value of helping others grow. The joy I feel is connected to the fulfillment of seeing someone evolve and succeed."[43]

How Can You Apply What You've Learned Here?

Understanding the "why" underlying your passion can shine light on the bigger potential area of personal growth that is available for your development down the road. It can open your eyes to how to continue growing and developing your passion, as well as the core values that may be tied in with it. It also will help you with your visioning activities in terms of the potentially broader scope of "who" and "what" you will focus on.

Closing Thoughts

Thanks for embarking on this passion-filled journey! In the next exercise, we'll tie it all together and explore how your values, skills, and passions intertwine to shape your authentic self. Your journey is unfolding beautifully, and it will be exciting to see where it leads.

EXERCISE 4
EXPLORE YOUR AUTHENTIC SELF

This challenge gets to the heart of your authentic self. Let's begin with what really floats your boat—just naturally. Consider what makes you feel good, what makes you feel present, happy, and grounded.

➤ **Find a comfy place to sit. Close your eyes. Take a few deep breaths to get into your own grounded rhythm and flow.**

➤ **When you're ready, open your eyes.**

➤ **Write down whatever immediately pops into your head when you read the following. Don't overthink it!**

1. When you really need to get back to yourself and feel like you're on solid ground (i.e., on a sturdy foundation), which of your values do you turn to for guidance and direction? This is a **GROUNDING VALUE**.

2. When you have a spare block of time, what is the first thing you typically do with that time (i.e., something you are continually drawn to and that is easy for you to do)? This is a **SPONTANEOUS SKILL**.

3. List a specific time in your life when you've felt completely content, and living truly in the present. Perhaps this involved doing the type of activity I refer to as a real "cobweb clearer," when you get into the flow and don't really think about anything else when you are doing it. Note down some details about that activity, the circumstances, and the feeling it generated. This is a **COBWEB-CLEARING PASSION.**

Taking these three core motivations together:

- Do you see any connections?
- Did you have any "aha" moments about how they might relate?
- Do you notice any links here to what you identified about your values, skills, and passions in Exercises 1 to 3? If so, what seems salient? If not, how might those fit with what you've discovered here?

How Can You Apply What You've Learned Here?

In considering the relationships between the three core motivations you described above, you may find that the times when you feel the most fulfilled offer a link between one or more core values you hold dear and their expression through a favourite activity and/or skill.

The next time you feel yourself in a cobweb-clearing state of action, take a moment to snap a photo of yourself (and those with you), record a quick audio file, or write a couple of lines down in your journal to describe the sensation and why you felt the way you did. Little reminders go a long way to understanding how to not only recreate but grow these situations to become even more of a force in your life!

Closing Thoughts

Thanks for taking this enlightening journey into your authentic self! Before we leap into the final exercise in Pillar 1, I want to note that this process—particularly learning about the "authentic self"—can be time-intensive and bring much to the surface. Speaking with friends, family, mentors, coaches, or other professionals for advice is natural throughout this journey, and it is not only encouraged but recommended throughout, as you desire. Further, I invite you to congratulate yourself on taking the time to go through this series of exercises to deepen your self-understanding as a starting point for the flowering process that is about to begin.

EXERCISE 5
DEEPEN YOUR AUTHENTIC SELF

This exercise, a reflection, will enable you to review and resonate with what you've learned so far. Please get your notebook.

▷ **Quickly recap your main motivations.**
From the last exercises, which key motivations (values, skills, and passions) are currently driving your authentic self?

▷ **Choose one word or a phrase to capture at least one key motivation driving your authentic self from each of these three motivational categories** (values, skills, passions).

▷ **Make a grid.**
Create a grid (see example, following) with three columns, listing the key motivator categories down the left side and the word/phrase for each listed in the centre column.

▷ **List ways to deepen your level of involvement with each key motivation.**
Is there a way you can expand the motivations that are most important for you? Is there a way to learn new things that can help you to increase your engagement with them? In the right-hand column, list at least three potential "expansions" for each main motivator that you would like to work on over the next year.

Key Motivator	Word or Phrase	Three Potential Focus Areas for Expansion
		I would like to develop …
		I would like to learn about …
		I would like to see …
A Key Value	Friendship	… my closest relationships
		… how to grow my network
		… an old friend
A Key Skill	Problem-Solving	… my chess-playing skills
		… new chess openings
		… a live chess tournament
A Key Passion	Dancing	… my partnering skills
		… ballet (a new form of dance for me)
		… a production of *Swan Lake* for inspo

> ### How Can _You_ Expand?
>
> My mom, after retiring, motivated by creativity as a grounding value, expanded her focus by signing up for a pottery class.
>
>

HOW CAN YOU APPLY WHAT YOU'VE LEARNED HERE?

As shown in the featured example, as my mom was better able to put a finger on a grounding value she was passionate about, she began to delve into more activities like gardening and knitting that deepened her involvement with creativity in meaningful ways.

We will see in the next part of the FUN Re-Visioning process that developing and investing in key motivators will help build your energy for taking things to an even greater level.

Closing Thoughts

Today, we have focused on how to take the best of yourself, from your current motivational framework, and work on deepening these aspects through your practices and engagements. Essentially, you are trying to create alignment between what you value, what you're good at, and what excites you.

That's it—you've completed the Foundations pillar of the **FUN Re-Visioning** process! Before jumping to Pillar 2, Uncovering, I recommend a break period of at least one week for personal reflection. Journalling can be especially helpful throughout this process, and I have provided some prompts to assist you during this personal reflection time.

— BREAK —
for Personal Reflection

In addition to taking a break before starting Pillar 2, if you have time, I suggest doing some journalling about your past. This is a great activity for getting some reflections down on paper—including how and why you are retiring or have retired—and can be VERY cathartic.

A friend, who is an author and a writing professor, suggested to me:

> Write like nobody is watching—get it all out. This is the very essence of journalling. Journalling in this form can serve to help you think clearly about what's worked in the past to bring you into more alignment with your aspirations ... Journalling is a way of resurfacing stories, ideas, thoughts, and experiences, and maybe even falling on an "aha" moment, an epiphany that can happen when we give ourselves permission to write without stopping to edit or judge. So, as such, journalling can be a clarifying exercise, a way to better understand who we are, what we do, and why we do it.[44]

My own experience was that journalling served as a launching pad to think deeply about how I wanted to live moving forward after my retirement. My friend's advice is so attuned with the endeavour of re-visioning your future that I felt it was important to share here.

So, as you take a little break for personal reflection, here are some thoughts and questions to ponder:

1. As far back as you can remember, what did you aspire to? An early memory.

2. Now, think of yourself as an onion. Each layer represents a different age or stage. Break the onion into five layers starting at the centre with your earliest memory listed above. Who you are today is made up, for example, of your inner selves at 16, 21, 35, 55, and all the meaningful times in between. Take some time and make a list of the stages of your life you remember best. Go back to each stage and, without overthinking, answer these questions as you might have done at each of those stages:

   - What was next?
   - What did I aspire to?
   - What legacy did I want to leave behind?

3. Make a list of three times you felt really stuck, when you didn't know what to do next or how to move forward. Once you've made that list, note how you moved forward (and reflect on the fact that you did, indeed, move forward!) and what you learned.

This reflective process can be emotional, so be kind and gentle with your former and current selves.

4. Now that you have spent some time reflecting on your past, it's time to journal about what the future might hold, from where you stand right now.

- What's next?
- What do you aspire to?
- What will your legacy be?

PILLAR 2
Uncovering (Week 2)

YOUR ASPIRATIONAL SELF

The five exercises of this second pillar probably represent the most important leap you can make between where you are now and your future. That future is your aspirational self—that vision-fuelled version of yourself that you dream of becoming.

A big question many people ask is where to start looking when you are trying to better know and understand your aspirational self. One of the most important things to recognize at the starting point of your journey is that the seeds for understanding your aspirational self already exist within you—you don't have to look far. As such, you may already have an inkling of what you are aspiring to do or to be. Sometimes, however, the journey toward your aspirational self can be surprising, as it has been buried beneath many layers of obligation and activity. So now, at the beginning of this next chapter, it's time for your aspirations to be uncovered and nurtured.

Two Paths to Your Aspirational Self

You can uncover your aspirational self in two ways:

1. Unintentional. One pathway is unintentional and can occur through (a) an epiphany—inspiration or an "aha" type of moment; or (b) recognizing recurring patterns within ourselves over time.

2. Intentional. The other pathway is more intentional: it's proactively seeking inspiration toward uncovering your aspirational self. Being proactive basically means acting to create or stimulate change rather than waiting and responding to circumstances as they arise.

The intentional process, or proactive inspiration, can involve actively scanning for ideas, or deep-diving your emotions, thoughts, motivations (values, skills, passions), or connection to spirit—as you are doing with this FUN Re-Visioning challenge.

Or you may start with a gut feeling or something that piques your interest—an unintentional start (i.e., you get inspired!)—and decide to follow up on this intentionally. The proactive part involves then spending time asking yourself or the universe questions, listening actively, and paying close attention to any answers you receive to take the ideas further.

The interesting thing, I find, is that the more you work on the intentional type of process, the more the unintentional process tends to happen. In other words, actively thinking about connections and motivations, over time, may lead to more epiphanies and "aha" moments.

Of course, the intentional path to aspirational discovery may involve some work. So, if you haven't already had an epiphany or "aha" in your life, to help you begin uncovering your aspirational self, let's see if you can be proactively inspired in that direction—through actively seeking patterns, ideas, insights, and intuitions.

EXERCISE 6
DISCOVER ASPIRATIONAL VALUES

One framework that can help you think about value development is Abraham Maslow's hierarchy of needs.[45] You may already be familiar with this theory, but here's a recap: Maslow suggests that only once the bottom fundamentals of the hierarchy are met (physiological needs like shelter, food, air, water, and sleep, as well as safety and security needs) can one move or evolve to the next steps up the pyramid to the realms of "love and belonging," "self-esteem," and ultimately something called "self-actualization," regarded as "the fulfillment of one's greatest potential."[46]

The aspirational values you decide to explore may be things that you have not focused on in the past. Or the values may be things you are aware of but want to bring more fully into your life.

▷ **Consider some aspirational values.**

1. Take a look at some aspirational values and think about which ones feel potentially important to you and how you might enhance or expand them in your life. For example, you may feel drawn to focusing on:

    relationships
    social values
    social justice

the environment

spirituality

morality

creativity

learning

innovativeness

openness

acceptance

freedom

well-being

... or something not listed here!

These are values which you may not have had enough time for in the past but might consider now as areas of focus. Now that you're in, or approaching, the next chapter of your life, you may have more time to take a second look to ensure that you're not leaving anything important on the table.

2. Write down your top three values from the list you've created that immediately appeal to you.

3. Looking for more ideas? Perhaps, look back to your Prep Exercise to see the three broad personal development themes you identified as potentially of interest.

> **Pick one aspirational value to focus on for now.**

1. Begin with a brief relaxation exercise—like breathing or movement—to ground yourself.

2. Close your eyes and ask yourself the following question: "What is the main aspirational value I will move forward with at this time?"

3. Write down the first word that pops into your mind without judging it. Consider this as a potential aspirational focal point to help in this stage of your re-visioning process and in your life.

How Can You Apply What You've Learned Here?

Picking one aspirational value that feels inspiring offers a starting place and a nudge toward beginning the next phase of the re-visioning process. Don't worry whether this aspirational value represents your soul's purpose for the rest of your life. Many people worry at this stage about "picking the right one." First, there may be more than one aspirational value involved with driving your purpose, but sometimes it's easiest to begin with one focal point. Second, please remember that we are all in a constant state of re-tuning, re-framing, and re-visioning, with our North Star continuing to come into focus. Why? Because outside circumstances—opportunities and challenges—continue to change in our lives and offer us different vantage points from which to see how to continue on our path. Third, part of this journey is about learning how to do the visioning thing! This, so you can keep applying it—the more you try it, the better you get at it. If it helps, you can think of the aspirational value you were inspired to pick with this exercise as one which offers you a warm-up lap, and one which will help with any future laps to come.

Closing Thoughts

Your aspirational self holds the key to defining or redefining your vision. Explore, reflect on, and embrace the values that resonate with your future. You are at the beginning of a beautiful new journey! Ride the wave of excitement you feel while discovering this!

EXERCISE 7
NAME IT

Today, we focus on making a connection between your authentic self, where you currently stand, and your aspirational self, where you aim to move toward in the future. The image that comes to mind is of a bridge, linking two worlds. Crossing that bridge can often be a challenging part of the re-visioning journey. So let's start with something simple.

▶ **Visualize aspirational you and name that aspiration to better connect with it.**

Start with the one aspirational value you noted down as a potential focal point in the previous exercise—one you want to build more of into your life.

1. Find a simple but meaningful single word that relates that value to you (feel free to use more words if better for you, but simplicity is key for remembering and reiterating). Don't let anything you haven't done or thought about before be a barrier. Keep yourself wide open.

2. Write your word down in huge letters on a sticky note and put it on your computer or bathroom mirror (or somewhere else you will see it often): "I'M (A/N) _____!"

Here are some examples:

Aspirational Value	I am (a/an) ...
Learning new things	Learner
Pursuing a spiritual journey	Spiritual
Mentoring	Mentor
Writing a book	Writer
Gaining financial independence	Independent

➢ **Adapt the example to fit your learning style.**
If you are a visual learner, you may find it helpful to quickly sketch an illustration that captures the essence of the word you have chosen. If you are a kinesthetic learner, you might feel the urge to create a model of what the word represents for you, or you may want to actually try out your word on a limited basis.

I'm a Runner!

When I turned 40, I wanted to run a marathon but had not run much since university. After I decided to do it, I tried to run 1 kilometre (just over half a mile) down the road with my daughter, but I needed to turn back and walk home before the halfway mark—no joke! I needed to figure out a way to convince myself that this dream wasn't nuts. I had read in a running magazine that you should start calling yourself a runner, even before you really feel like one. So I did that. I started telling people I was a runner, and it did feel a bit weird at first. Or, as a recent focus group participant mentioned, when she named "it," she felt like she had "imposter syndrome." This is totally normal! But in my case, gradually, as I kept saying it and as I kept progressing, it became a reality. That first 42-kilometre (26-mile) marathon took me over 5 hours on a sweltering day in Paris—but I did it and I was thrilled! I WAS a runner!

How Can You Apply What You've Learned Here?

I want you to have fun with naming "it," a key aspiration for yourself! Be as creative as possible and don't hold back in terms of the abundant possibilities that lie before you. Not only can you try representing your word using your different modalities, you may even try out a variety of names to get at the underlying essence of what you want it to stand for.

Closing Thoughts

You've worked hard to gain a better understanding of how your authentic and aspirational selves can come together and operate as the foundation for building a vision for your future. Well done!

CONGRATULATIONS! YOU'RE ALMOST HALFWAY THERE!

EXERCISE 8
ACTIVATE: ATTITUDE

In the last two exercises, we've talked about uncovering a key value you would like to pursue as part of your overall aspirational self you are moving toward and as a focal point for the re-visioning exercises in this workbook. Many people speak of seeking a single purpose toward which they direct all activities—some people are directed primarily in one way; others have multiple purposes which they would like to explore or possibly even eventually link together, as they grow their aspirational self. Whichever the case for you, we're now going to look at the internal development work you can start doing to get energized for that growth.

Most fledgling ideas have certain things in common that they need to be able to thrive—and essentially, these "thrive mechanisms" are all about activating energy. And activating energy is about what I call the **triple-A energy drivers**:

- Attitude
- Alignment
- Amplification

Exercises 8, 9, and 10 of our week with FUN Re-Visioning Pillar 2 focus on each in turn.

ATTITUDE: OPENING YOUR MIND

When we talk about good attitude, we often mean having an open mind toward learning. As you will recall, from the beginning of the workbook, I drew your attention to the importance of mindset when it comes to success with visioning. Believing in your own potential for development acts as a strong motivator. Psychology professor Carol Dweck terms this a "growth mindset."[47]

People who have a growth mindset trust that they are capable of reaching their goals, and if not, they also trust that they will be able to develop or obtain whatever skills or resources are required to get them there. These people enhance their ability to persistently access abundance through actions like working hard, networking, reading, gaining access to good teachers and mentors, and, yes, opening up to new ideas and strategies for guiding their lives. They also know the power of setting an intention and believing they will achieve it.

An open attitude is a prerequisite for activating purpose. It requires operating at our highest possible frequency to gain as much openness as possible. To that end, there are various mind, body, and spirit practices that can help with developing more openness.

According to the practice of chi gong—*chi* meaning "life force" or "energy"—there are two states of being: opening and closing. In other words, we generally operate in a state of either expansion or contraction. And we all know the difference in how these two states feel—how it feels to be open- or closed-hearted about new people, situations, or ideas. The state of expansiveness or opening is the state that is associated with higher-level and positive energy, resulting in well-being, abundance, and growth.

> **Experiment with cultivating openness.**

It is difficult to will ourselves to higher states of energy through the mind alone. Tapping into the body and soul can be gateways to removing blockages and enhancing flow, leading to more openness and expansion. Practices known to help with this include:

- Meditation (many apps are available to help you start)
- Vibrational sound practices (chanting, drumming, gong baths)
- Slow, repetitive physical activity (long walks, gardening)
- Practices to relax you (massage, sauna, hot baths)
- Time in nature
- Dancing, singing, listening to music
- Baking, cooking
- Cleaning and decluttering (yes, for some people—myself included—it works!)
- Relaxation or energy rebalancing exercises (yoga, tai chi, deep breathing, tapping, reiki)
- Supporting good causes
- Socializing
- Gratitude practices

How Can You Apply What You've Learned Here?

If you haven't already done so, I encourage you to try a number of the above practices to see which one(s) work for you. If possible, one easy place to start is simply by aiming to spend 20 minutes outside each day. Once you find one or more opening practices that you gravitate to and that work for you, try to build them into your life on a regular and ongoing basis.

Closing Thoughts

Cultivate openness and positive energy to foster more purposeful growth!

EXERCISE 9
ACTIVATE: ALIGNMENT

In Exercise 7, you identified an aspirational value you would like to explore more and described your aspirational self by naming it (for example, "I'm a learner"). But you may have yet to figure out how to manifest that value in the world you want to see.

Getting your aspirational self to "light up" likely involves learning about new things and developing new skills and practices. It also requires thinking about how to *align* it with your life and your current values (your authentic self). Understanding how to do this requires work, time, and energy so that what you focus on and align with becomes more and more visible in your mind's eye. In today's exercise, you take one of the first key steps in turning your aspiration into reality: developing a homework plan.

ALIGNMENT: DOING YOUR HOMEWORK

Doing upfront homework about what your own path might look like is the equivalent of an entrepreneur, before pursuing a market opportunity, doing an industry deep dive or conducting market research. Doing this type of background research also applies outside of the business world. It is equally important, when personally re-visioning, to familiarize yourself with your "subject of study" to see which ideas, opportunities, or possibilities out there strike a chord with your interests, values, and strengths (both authentic and aspirational).

Note: This kind of upfront homework can take some time.

Sometimes it's hard to know where to start—especially when you're on a new path you don't know much about. I've found that breaking things down into bite-sized pieces always helps with this process. You will learn how to do that in the exercise below.

STARTING FROM "SCRATCH"

Choreographer Twyla Tharp, in her book *The Creative Habit*, has a very cool way of referring to the process of conducting upfront homework for inspiration, as applied in creative pursuits. She calls it "scratching ... what you do when you don't want to wait for the thunderbolt to hit you."[48] Tharp gives examples from various artistic professions—"a fashion designer is scratching when he visits vintage clothing stores ... a film director is scratching when she grabs a flight to Rome ... an architect is scratching when he walks through a rock quarry."[49]

So what might "scratching" look like for you? What do you do when you feel the need for inspiration? Is there somewhere you like to be in your house or workspace to tackle new projects? Is there somewhere you like to visit that is particularly inspiring to you? Are there people in your network who inspire you when you get together? Are there things you like to do that help you get in the zone or make you feel more creative? Maybe you like to get a little out of your comfort zone, cook a new recipe, try a new dance, or listen to new music. Are there teachers, coaches, or experts who might be able to help you?

When I thought about writing a screenplay related to this book, for example, a friend suggested watching Aaron Sorkin's MasterClass on screenwriting. It was very inspiring and gave me ideas for software and tools I could use, as well as processes that would be helpful for getting started.

Bite-Sized Pieces

One of my big aspirational goals over the last couple of years has been to live my life more consciously as a spiritual journey. There were so many places I could have started, yet the topic that intrigued me the most was Buddhism. That said, I knew very little when I got started. So, in order to avoid becoming overwhelmed with all the information out there on the topic, I chose three Buddhist principles—core tenets of the philosophy—to focus on. I felt these would get me on the kind of path I wanted to follow, and I could break them down further to help move forward with more specific goal-setting.

The three core principles I decided to focus on and learn more about were:

1. Letting go of attachments
2. Putting yourself in other people's shoes
3. Giving back

I knew there would be much more to learn, but you have to start somewhere. So, I focused on principles that intuitively appealed to me and felt important for serving my ultimate aspiration to help others with their visions.

In other words, you need to set some short-term, vision-driven goals that make sense for helping you to reach your longer-term vision.

If possible, put into words what you want to ask or know as clearly as possible. When I started doing research on Buddhism, for example, I asked myself, "How do I put myself in other people's shoes?" I soon came across the "rope trick" as outlined by Geshe Michael Roach and Lama Christie McNally in *The Diamond Cutter*.[50] This helpful tool encourages empathy and is now a core practice I am trying to build into my daily life. (The rope trick involves standing next to another person, imagining you tie yourselves together with a rope and become one person. The aim is to imagine that as one person, your reactions, responses, and interactions involve this blended being.)

So writing down your questions can help you better understand what you seek with your homework, plan your research path accordingly, and secure some tools and strategies to get you on your path. This doesn't mean it's always easy or comes naturally, but somehow when I'm in a situation feeling "closed" to empathy, all I need to do is think of the words "rope trick" and it opens me up! No kidding!

> **Build your homework plan.**

1. Choose one core area of research, or core topic, that immediately appeals to you, related to your aspiration. You can aim to delve into your homework plan and learn more about this topic over the next three months—or even longer. The timing will depend on your schedule and ability to gain information on the topic and is something you can elaborate on more once you've finished the workbook. Don't worry about whether you are starting on the best or most important thing first—you need to jump in somewhere, and doing so will naturally lead to gaining a better picture of the overall field of your interest. The idea here is to build a plan to begin studying the topic that is immediately of interest to you.

2. Next, think about three core principles, areas of focus, disciplines, building blocks, or audiences within your area of interest which appeal to you to research and learn more about. You may already have some in mind, or doing the research may bring something to light you had never thought of before. For example, if you are interested in mentoring, you might start by researching what types of mentoring programs there are. Say one area that appeals to you from this initial research is mentoring children. Then you might want to dig further into biographies, research, or stories about people mentoring children in three different ways: for example, you might focus on children in a Big Brothers Big Sisters type of program, children with learning challenges, or children

with an interest in your own area of expertise. Write down your three core principles/areas using a chart like the one following.

Aspirational Value	I am (a/an)	Core Topic	Three Core Principles/ Focus Areas
			I want to do this by learning about/focusing on
Learning new things	Learner	History of education	Different educational systems
			Education success stories
			How to be a good learner
Pursuing a spiritual journey	Spiritual	Buddhist philosophy	Letting go
			Being in other people's shoes
			Giving back
Writing a book	Writer	How to get published	Creating a book plan
			Different ways to publish
			Different genres
Gaining financial independence	Independent	Financial planning	Finding a financial adviser
			Developing an abundance mentality
			Creating a financial plan

3. Dig in and do some research! This may include:

   - Looking up some history on the topic as well as related topics in the news
   - Tapping into books, articles, videos, podcasts, courses, and online sources of pertinent information
   - Contacting experts
   - Talking to other people interested in the topic
   - Reaching out to relevant associations or groups involved with the topic

For example, are you trying to figure out how to get the energy to focus on a new direction? Then take the time to learn about methods for doing this. Research energy-raising techniques, and learn about and engage in new practices known to do so that appeal to you.

Or are you trying to figure out how to finance a vision you feel is out of reach? Connecting with people who do have this knowledge (either directly or through their writing, research, or social media) and making a plan for the financials behind your vision will be part of your homework.

How Can You Apply What You've Learned Here?

The key with this exercise is to break down the core topic you've identified relating to your aspirational value. The idea is to take small steps toward your aspirational goal by making it more approachable. To do so, gain more information and insights through conducting your homework on the subtopics you've identified. Then fine-tune and rejig your plan as you go along.

There are specific questions you might ask in a moment of quiet thought, meditation, or prayer in order to help you understand "what more do I need and want to learn about these topics?" What pieces of the puzzle might you like to fill in, or who might you want to speak with to help you on your way? Seeking further clarification to better know what you don't yet know will bring many ideas, people, and opportunities your way.

Closing Thoughts

Paulo Coelho suggests that "when someone makes a decision, [they are] really diving into a strong current that will carry [them] to places [they] had never dreamed of when [they] first made the decision."[51]

EXERCISE 10
ACTIVATE: AMPLIFICATION

"Amplification" means taking what you understand so far about your authentic and aspirational self and pumping up the level of detail to clarify what you know. For this, I have found drawing a mind map to be one of the most effective—and enjoyable!—approaches to taking self-awareness to the next level.

AMPLIFICATION: MIND MAPPING

A mind map is a visual representation of a concept you have in your head. This visual map gets updated as you continue connecting with others and doing your homework on your topic. Your thought process is an organic one and grows through distinction-making, or seeing things in finer-grained detail, an ability which you gain as you learn more about a topic. Doing so, in turn, enables you to continue clarifying your thinking around the basic concept of your aspiration and seeing it in relation to your authentic self.

Having a visual in front of you enables a big-picture look at the foundational components of yourself you have outlined thus far—how they relate to you, your activities, and one another. It offers a starting point.

Then, elaborating your mind map with the amplification process offers a basis for reflection and enables you to continue building ideas out further as you move through re-visioning. This enhances your understanding of your aspiration and the direction it's taking you in, to help you form a vision to bring that aspiration to life. You want to capture not only the core aspects of your aspirational self that will help fire up your vision, but also the elements of your authentic self—those values, skills, and passions that already make you who you are and help fuel your energy level to bridge to your aspiration. In other words, it's important to see both aspects, your authentic and aspirational selves, in the mind map.

▷ **Create a mind map.**

1. Draw yourself in the middle of the page.
2. Label the left side of the page "Authentic Self" and the right side "Aspirational Self."
3. On the left, list as many components of your authentic self as you like (values, skills, passions) in different bubbles, grouping things that hang together.
4. On the right, in a bubble, list your aspiration from Exercise 7, along with the core topic from Exercise 9 that you are focusing on. Coming out from that, draw an additional bubble in which you will write the three core principles from Exercise 9 you want to learn more about.
5. If you already have a vision of where you want to move to, or were moving in a certain direction when you began this process, write words that capture that above your head. If not, don't worry—we'll be covering that with the Pillar 3 exercises.

RE-VISIONING RETIREMENT

My Mind Map

A mind map doesn't need to make sense to anyone else. It's just fun—and useful—to get it all down on the page, a place to visualize your thoughts. Below is the version of the mind map I created for myself at this stage.

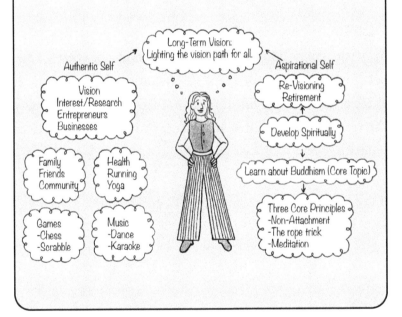

How Can You Apply What You've Learned Here?

After the next break period, in Pillar 3, you will use your mind map as you flesh out your vision for the future, by continuing to add detail as your thoughts around your authentic and aspirational selves and your vision continue to deepen and become clearer.

Closing Thoughts

Your starter mind map is a great summary of what you've accomplished through FUN Re-Visioning Pillars 1 and 2. Congratulations on all of your hard work thus far! Enjoy the feeling of connecting in an authentic, energized way to your future!

— BREAK —
for Guided Reflection

To help you think about the work you've done in Pillars 1 and 2 to understand your authentic and aspirational selves better, and in preparation for bridging to creating a vision, I suggest first taking some time off from the exercises to let things marinate, perhaps continuing with the homework process (Exercise 9) and any openness practices you have found useful (see Exercise 8).

Then to pick up momentum again, once you are ready, I offer you a three-part Networking Exercise. It takes time to create meaningful networks, so the idea is to get you thinking about who you may want to connect with once you have finished the workbook and begin implementing your vision.

If you would like to keep the rhythm of your weekly five-day practice, I suggest the following schedule.

▸ Break Day 1

Play catch-up with any homework you want to make time for or exercises you may have wanted to flesh out more. You also might consider going back to the Prep Exercise and reflecting on how your original three broad themes relate to the direction you are moving in now. These may not necessarily map out onto each other now—not to worry! Continue with the direction you have struck out in and note how you might want to incorporate the original themes into where you are heading: Where might they sit in your mind map?

▸ Break Day 2

Read "**From Aspirational Value to Vision: A Little More about My Story**" on the facing page.

▸ Break Days 3, 4, and 5

Get ready for Pillar 3, which starts to put your vision into action, by completing the three-part **Networking Exercise** following the story.

From Aspirational Value to Vision: A Little More about My Story

I would like to share more about my personal story as an example of FUN Re-Visioning in action. It offers a sneak peek at how the exercises we have already done may tie into the exercises to come.

Becoming a Student Again (Attitude)

In early 2022, as I was going through my own re-visioning exercise and doing self-work to open myself up to my aspirations, I realized that for a long time I had been "the teacher." And what I was craving was to be "the student" again—specifically, I wanted to be a student on a spiritual journey (my aspirational value!). I wanted to access novel ideas and information from new and different types of teachers. I wanted to actively grow my network in new directions to help renew my vision and ultimately experience a meaningful journey moving forward.

Part of what I believe I was searching for, in re-visioning and carving a new path toward becoming a student again, was learning how to be more open. I wanted to learn how to connect freely with others without fear, using my feeling abilities and not just my

Continued...

thinking abilities. This was an outcome I was looking to achieve—more focus on feeling and intuition—as thinking my way through things had been my go-to for a long time! By doing so, I hoped to enhance my ability to give back to others and deliver on my desire to help others find a path for developing their own vision.

Picking My Focal Topic to Develop an Aspirational Value ... or Having One Picked for Me (Alignment)

This is a true story—of the epiphany sort. As I was thinking about and writing an early draft of this book, I looked over at my bookshelf. One book seemed strangely out of place, jutting forward as if willing me to pick it up. So I did.

The book was called *The Diamond Cutter*[52]—I had picked it up on one of my visits to Kripalu, a retreat in the Berkshires of Massachusetts. The book had probably been recommended by one of the speakers who led sessions there. Despite being interested enough to purchase it several years earlier, I had never even cracked its spine. As I often do, I read the last section of the book first—I know—double-duty spoiler alert. But I find it useful to see where the author is heading

Continued...

before delving into a book (that is, what their vision is in writing the book and what they want to teach me).

And there it was, in the very first paragraph of the epilogue. The authors, Geshe Michael Roach and Lama Christie McNally, had written: "A lot of the information in this little book is wisdom that has been passed on over the centuries mainly by word of mouth, from teacher to student, deep within the Buddhist monasteries of Tibet and India ... Putting into actual practice all the instructions here ... is something that you can do much better with the guidance of a living teacher."[53] The words leapt off the page at me.

Indeed, these words helped me realize that as a student, I was looking for new spiritual teachers, those who could help lift me out of my singularly driven achievement mindset into something else—something more focused on collective energy, something more open to others, something that would help me to be more present and heart-centred. The nudge from *The Diamond Cutter* seemed exactly what I needed. The words of Roach, as he described his experience, seemed to speak directly to me. I even liked his writing style and the fact that he seemed to "get" me and my desire to somehow combine spirituality and the business world.

Continued...

RE-VISIONING RETIREMENT

So "now we're ready to get down to brass tacks," he says. "Admit it. You want to be good in business ... but you also have a strong instinct that tells you life wouldn't be much unless it had a spiritual side to it."[54] The book inspired me to look through a specific lens at the topic of spirituality—that of Buddhism.

My aspirational journey had begun. Not only had I pinpointed an aspirational value I wanted to work on (becoming a student of spirituality), but I also had a core topic I wanted to learn more about (Buddhist philosophy).

RE-FOCUSING MY EFFORTS AS A TEACHER (AMPLIFICATION)

So how did I begin amplifying my new vision? I started with outlining three core principles of Buddhism that immediately appealed to me (as shown in Exercise 9: letting go, putting yourself in other people's shoes, giving back) to work on improving my understanding.

And then I revisited my long-standing vision, which was to help others with their own visioning. I had worked with businesses and entrepreneurs to help them develop their own vision statements, but when I thought of the greater need in society it became apparent to me that my calling stood with individuals, and the greatest number

Continued...

of those individuals were in the 50+ age bracket. The community I immediately identified with was what I sometimes refer to as the NARLYs: the newly and about-to-be retired (in some cases leaving the workforce young).

I knew that refocusing in a truly authentic way meant putting myself in the shoes of these people I was trying to better understand by listening to their stories and spending time with them. That is exactly what I have spent the last few years doing. The findings from my primary research involving interviews and focus groups with the NARLYs were applied when I fleshed out the exercises and content of this workbook.

In terms of published work (i.e., secondary sources), there is a wealth of material focused on health, advocacy, travel planning, and financial advice. Additionally, I found several studies that showed finding purpose was important for positive health outcomes, as noted in the Introduction to this workbook. That said, however, I found no specific work on the topic of visioning for this audience—and, importantly, this was a perspective I believed that I had the expertise to share.

After doing my homework, I felt that the ideas for working closely with kindred spirit retirees, as well as somehow grounding my approach in Buddhism, had

Continued...

emerged as my "riffs," to borrow from Twyla Tharp's lingo. These were the building blocks for my vision: I hoped to take my existing knowledge and visioning tools, developed for organizations and entrepreneurs, and find ways to apply them for the benefit of retirees. I felt so stoked when I thought about the possibilities.

In sum, I had decided that I wanted to begin a spiritual quest and also learn more about retirement and retirees and how I might bring these aspects together with a re-visioning process. For me, going on a spiritual journey as a learner with fresh eyes and heart was going to be an important part of my developing story. I decided to set out along that path, to learn how to be inspired, and then perhaps be able to give back to the NARLY community. I was beginning to understand that my own aspiration and resulting re-visioning were going to be related to figuring out what that path might look like for NARLYs like me.

NETWORKING EXERCISE

This exercise is meant to be conducted over the next three days (Days 3, 4, and 5) of your guided reflection period. Locate your pen and notebook and get ready to plug into the energy, support, and guidance that networking offers.

Everyone's journey is unique, just like their fingerprints. That said, the need for connectivity, in a more general sense, may be a common denominator, particularly during one's re-visioning years. Connectivity can involve communing with one's spiritual side, but it may also simply mean being open to new ideas or relationships. And this is effectively one of the most important things I have learned through speaking with people on my own re-visioning journey: regardless of our unique path we seek, in the end it's about connection.

Focusing on connection, this three-part networking exercise will help you bring your vision forward to the world once you finish this workbook.

CONNECT THROUGH NETWORKING

Some things in life you can't control. But some things you can, and among the most important of these is surrounding yourself with people who are willing to help you move the needle on realizing your life's vision. This might seem obvious, or just common sense. It is, but research findings have also shown that it's true. My own PhD research, for example, showed that networking is one of the key elements that can have a positive impact on effective visioning.

Suffice to say, creating and implementing a vision on your own can be challenging, but if you surround yourself and engage with the resources of a really solid network of people, you will greatly improve your chances of achieving a satisfying vision. In other words, the social context in which your vision unfolds counts. Delegating some of your personal network of family, friends, and mentors to be part of an informal visioning team is one of the most important things you can focus on when bringing your vision to fruition. It's vital to think about how you would like to actively grow this existing network as well—yes, even in the next chapter of your life—to connect with new people to help you realize your goals.

DEVELOP THREE KEY NETWORKS

We're going to think about how to develop a three-pronged network to support your visioning journey: first, through assembling what I call your "visioning team"; second, through working with colleagues interested in similar aspirational goals; and third, through finding experts in the field.

➤ **1. Break Day 3: Create a visioning team.**
Creating a visioning team is a good way to help keep you focused on your vision. Your visioning team can be as small as you and your life partner, closest family member, or best friend, or much larger than that.

A **logical first question to ask** yourself is: "Who in my network should be part of my visioning team?" Specifically, "Who might be able to help me develop my vision further and achieve it?"

Put together a potential list for your visioning team. The most obvious place to start is with people who really care about your well-being and know about your strengths and weaknesses, as well as your skills and values. For example, you might consider including the following types of individuals:

- Family members and close friends
- Influential teachers, coaches, guides
- Financial advisers, community leaders, spiritual leaders
- Trusted current and former bosses and colleagues

In considering this team, **think of people who can be beneficial as a sounding board** and provide the time necessary for serious brainstorming and rational analysis (i.e., not just saying "Sounds good to me!"). Effectively, then, a visioning team is a dynamic group of people, closely tied to you in some capacity, who have specific mentoring capabilities. Qualities to look for in your visioning team include the ability and willingness to

- keep you on point in terms of sustaining your authentic self while continuing to support your growing interests on your aspirational side,

- challenge you to ask good questions and help reformulate your thinking when required,
- push your idea-championing skills,
- assist you with further networking,
- offer expertise when possible, and
- perhaps most importantly, be a good cheerleader!

Given these points, who would you really like to include on this list? Then create a list where you **specifically note why each of these people should be on your visioning team.**

Then, based on availability and your final selection of people, you might **conduct an interview** (either in person, on the phone/internet, or through e-mail) with each person. You might want to send each person some open-ended questions to get them thinking before you meet with them. Here are some **suggested interview questions** as a starting point:

- I have listed X as a new aspiration to learn more about. How does this land with you?
- Any suggestions on how you might see this aligning with my life or how to learn more?
- Here are the three topics I am learning about related to this aspiration; are there any other topics you think I should look at that might be of interest to me?
- Here is the vision statement I have drafted [you will do this in FUN Pillar 3]. Any suggestions for re-visioning this?

- What short-term steps do you think will help me in moving toward this aspiration/vision?

Consulting your notes from each meeting or e-mail exchange, list three key takeaways from the exercise after a period of reflection.

Having explored today how to create a visioning team, during the next two days we're going to look at how to connect, in two ways, with individuals who have similar interests to yours.

▶ **2. Break Day 4: Tap into a collegial network.**
Colleagues offer another pool from which to draw networking support for your vision. This is where I started my own journey of networking over the last couple of years: by speaking with other people I knew who had just retired or were thinking of retiring and, like me, wanted to continue working on some level and wanted to give back based on their expertise. (Thank you, all of you who were part of my visioning team, as well as colleagues who contributed to my journey!)

To begin this process, list a few people who have similar interests and who either are at a similar stage of retiring as you, or are a little more advanced in the process.

Next, you might also look up and connect with people in a local association or group whom you've not necessarily met with before, but who have similar interests. For example, many people have the desire during this time in their lives to foster new creative pursuits, which they may not have had time or energy for in the past, such as learning to paint, taking up a musical instrument, or acting. Some universities offer courses specifically directed toward people who are "retired-ish" and looking at a next chapter or working more entrepreneurially. As just one example, a friend, who is part of my own visioning team, has started offering writing workshops at a local university to teach people how to write their own memoirs. Beyond classes, there might also be the possibility of joining a local amateur art co-op, band, choir, or theatre group, for example. These types of organizations are often looking for new, and perhaps unexplored, talent and like-minded individuals to join in.

List five people you know (or would like to get to know) who you think might make good potential colleagues and list why:

1.

2.

3.

4.

5.

Networking activity: List specific tools (e.g., social media), events, introductions (people that can help connect you), and groups that can be used to enhance your list and/or meet people on your list:

- Tools:
- Events:
- Introductions:
- Three possible associations that you can join/connect with or classes you might sign up for based on your interests:

    1.

    2.

    3.

▷ **3. Break Day 5: Seek out experts.**

Another way to consider expanding your network is to add different types of advisers with relevant expertise to further develop your own subject expertise and help you realize your vision. For example, notaries, bankers, financial advisers, real estate specialists, and lawyers may offer necessary support in terms of ensuring you have your ducks in a row financially and legally for pursuing your dreams. Adding in technical specialists, teachers, coaches, or others with appropriate expertise can help you develop your skills, ideas, and interests and move you more quickly to enacting the vision of your dreams.

List five experts or advisers you would like to discuss your ideas with. If you don't have a specific person in mind, you can simply list a job title or company or type of experience.

1.
2.
3.
4.
5.

Networking activity: List specific tools (e.g., social media), events, or introductions that can be used to enhance your list or ability to contact experts on your list.

- Tools:
- Events:
- Introductions:

Here are some **suggested interview questions** you might consider asking to learn more from an expert about a new field of interest (if relevant):

- Can you tell me a little about your background and how you got interested in this area?
- Are there key associations I can join or conferences/workshops I can attend to learn more? Do you offer any workshops?
- What publications should I read and what online sources should I check out to learn more?
- What are the most important aspects of what you are doing in terms of giving back (or other important aspects that align with your aspiration/vision)?
- Are there other experts you'd suggest I speak to?

PILLAR 3
Nurturing (Week 3)

YOUR VISIONARY SELF

The goal of these last five exercises of Pillar 3 is to crystallize all of the thinking and soul-searching you have done thus far into a vision statement. In other words, you are going to take all of the vision seeds you have sown and nurture them to bear the fruit you desire. And the best way to start bringing your vision to life is by creating a vision statement.

I want you to take a moment to pat yourself on the back for your dedication thus far to undertaking the re-visioning process! It has demanded a great deal of self-awareness and reflection, but at this stage you will have achieved several key milestones already. Let's recap. You have

- gained a clearer picture of your authentic self;
- identified ideas for enhancing your authentic self;
- developed ways to build your energy resources;
- built an understanding of your aspirational focus through attitude, alignment, and amplification; and
- created a visual mind map that connects these ideas and provides a focal point for the visioning process.

And now (drum roll!), you are ready to take all of this work and create a vision statement to encapsulate your thoughts, feelings, and desires in a way that expresses how you want to move forward with your aspirational goal!

Vision statements are excellent tools. They enable you to communicate your vision easily and confidently to yourself and others. This in turn allows things to get real by getting buy-in from others, creating accountability, and enhancing your desire to deliver on the vision. Numerous studies in the business world have shown the positive effects of vision statements on performance outcomes, and there is no reason to believe that it would be any different with personal vision statements. Creating your own personal vision statement will, at the very least, bring you to the next step of your journey, which, if driven by your desires and aspirations, will be a positive outcome in itself.

So Pillar 3 focuses on nurturing your nascent vision to create a clear, succinct, tangible vision statement that represents an aspirational direction that you plan to move toward in the future.

Before beginning this process, you might want to think back to the key activator values you noted down during the exercises focused on building self-awareness about your authentic self (Pillar 1). These can serve as a great catalyst for developing visioning strategies as a way to approach the next section.

THREE STRATEGIES FOR CONSTRUCTING A VISION STATEMENT

You can frame a vision statement using visioning strategies in three main ways:

1. **Target-based visioning** is a solid approach for those of you motivated by learning goal orientation and/or self-efficacy. A target date like "I will be travelling three months out of each year by 2028" offers an easy example of this type of vision and might appeal to those who like reaching specific milestones and doing so quickly and clearly, driven by their own efforts.

2. **Benchmark-based visioning** uses role modelling as a way to think about framing a vision statement. This can be an effective approach if you are driven, for example, by altruistic-biospheric values. Assertions like "I would like to give back to the world in the way that Mother Teresa did" or "I want to be the next big environmentalist à la Rachel Carson" are ways of using role models as analogies to think about potential process and impact when moving forward with such goals.

3. **Innovation-based visioning** is a great match if you are highly motivated by your own ability to innovate and/or be autonomous, or are a divergent thinker. This approach can serve as a subject-related framing mechanism for those interested in the arts and letters, sciences, and

other creative pursuits like painting, cooking, gardening: "I will allow myself the freedom to experiment with X."

Keeping these possible approaches in mind, in the next five exercises, you will begin the process of developing, testing, and solidifying a vision statement. Developing a vision statement requires first defining your vision goal's form and scope (Exercise 11), then drafting the core message that will underlie your vision (Exercise 12). You then need to test these initial vision statement elements to see how magnetic and clear they are for you at this stage (Exercise 13). Finally, you will solidify and polish your vision statement (Exercise 14) and draft your initial plan for bringing it to fruition (Exercise 15).

EXERCISE 11
DEFINE YOUR VISION GOAL

To flesh out some initial insights for your vision statement, the first natural focal point is the **vision goal—its form and scope** (see under "What Is Vision?" in the "Power of Vision" section earlier). Defining your vision's form and scope contributes to clarifying and enacting your aspiration.

Here, in Exercise 11, you will devote some time to quiet thought or meditation around specific questions to help you **express the overall concept** of your vision (that is, the goal—defined by its form and scope). Exercise 12 will help you better **define the message** behind your vision (and therefore, bring clarity to understanding how it will work). In Exercise 13, you will **test the strength** of your vision, in terms of how passionate you are about it and whether it is clear and specific enough for you to feel ready to move forward with it.

If you have some basic ideas for where you want to go with your vision but feel some pieces of the puzzle are still missing, think about

- what aspects of your aspirational value you don't know enough about yet,
- where you might seek more information or guidance, and
- who you might speak with to help you on your way—either physically or metaphysically.

The key is ensuring that the questions you ask are clear in the first place. Only then can you find, receive, or intuit clear answers.

So, for example, if you are trying to figure out what you need to know more about and are having trouble coming up with good questions, you might ask yourself:

- "What is showing up in my life that I've missed in the past?"
- "What is the most important thing for me to focus on now?"
- "How can I show myself what I want to do in the clearest way?"

> ### Ask to Receive
>
> In my case, I had begun to ask for clarity related to my post-retirement goals in a meditation exercise. I then discovered that what I was looking for as an aspiration was spiritual direction. Right after that experience, guidance started coming down the pipe and it felt like it was flowing. As described previously, I was led to understand that I wanted to be a student again and that my path was to learn more about Buddhism.

▷ **Define the form of your goal.**

As a reminder, the main aspects of form are:

- **Who** is involved (certainly you, but it might involve others as well)
- **What** the image actually looks like in your mind and what elements or building blocks are involved in bringing the image together
- **When** it will happen (if relevant)

1. Begin with a brief relaxation exercise—like breathing or movement—to ground yourself.
2. Think about each of the three aspects (who, what, when) in turn and compile a list of questions to ask yourself.
3. Here are some suggestions for questions.

"Who" questions:
- How do I fit into the picture, or what is my role in facilitating the goal?
- Who does this vision apply to? Just me or does it involve or affect others as well?

"What" questions:
- What are the key features, building blocks, or elements making up the form of my goal?
- How do the separate features look or feel when they come together in my vision?

- Are there interactions between various features that need to be considered?
- What does the environment in which the goal unfolds look like?
- Are there other elements that need to be in place for it to work?

"When" questions:
- Is there a specific timing that is critical to making my goal happen? (Is there a specific date by when I need or desire it to be achieved, or is there an external date I am working toward?)
- Does the goal of the vision enable the achievement of another goal? Is this a short-term goal related to a longer-term potential goal?

▷ **Define the scope of your goal.**
The main aspects of a goal's scope are:

- Its size or magnitude
- Its potential for impact
- The potential length of time necessary for its achievement

1. Begin with a brief relaxation exercise—like breathing or movement—to ground yourself.
2. Think about each of the three aspects in turn and compile a list of questions to ask yourself.
3. Here are some suggestions for questions:

   - Is this goal specifically applicable only to me?
   - To what extent does my goal potentially help others?
   - Does my goal contribute to improving conditions in the future (society, the environment)?
   - What is the potential to create value from the vision for myself or others?
   - Is there profit potential in this vision? If not, does that matter to me?
   - How long will it likely take to enact this goal? Or is it more of an ongoing thing?

How Can You Apply What You've Learned Here?

I recommend adding any ideas that come from these Pillar 3 exercises to your mind map (from Exercise 10). To help with this process, I suggest keeping a separate section of your notebook to log words, phrases, and ideas that come to mind at this stage which can be used to describe various attributes of your concept/goals. Jot them down in your notebook as they come to you. Then, in moments when you have more structured time, you can sit down and add them to your mind map in a more categorized way.

Closing Thoughts

Keep your notebook close at hand during this period of time. You have been asking many questions of yourself and of the universe to help clarify your overall concept, which will serve as the basis for defining your vision goal. The ideas are bound to start flowing and you want to capture as many of them as you can!

EXERCISE 12
DRAFT YOUR CORE MESSAGE

Based on the previous exercises, and your upfront homework, you likely now have some core ideas ready to assemble into your bigger vision picture. Next, you are going to use all of these nuggets to start crafting the core message underlying your vision.

> **Create a first draft of your core message.**

1. Begin by writing down a list of words or phrases describing key attributes of your aspiration from your most recent mind map, and from answers to the questions asked when fleshing out your vision goal (Exercise 11). You might even try putting words from your mind map, your homework research, and reflections into a word cloud generator (you can find many for free online) to create a visual to get your creative juices going. It's a way to see, in a free-flow manner, the words you tend to use when thinking about your values and aspirations, and it also highlights the words you use most—that is, those that are most salient and meaningful for you.

2. Write down some additional words, concepts, and ideas that really resonate with you and that you feel help, as much as possible, to convey your underlying thinking around your vision goal.

3. Group the words together in three to five sentences or phrases to convey a general sense of the message underlying your vision goal as clearly and concisely as possible.

4. Remove all motherhood statements. Most people want to be innovative, have good values, be a good citizen, and so on—get rid of all that stuff and just focus on the core that is specific to you.

5. Remove all jargon. The average person should be able to read the statement and understand what it means.

6. Shorten your message to, at most, one to three simple, straightforward sentences or phrases. Take a break and don't look at this draft again until you are ready to move on to the next exercise.

How Can You Apply What You've Learned Here?

The key after drafting your core message is to take a break from crafting it. Put it aside for now. We will come back to continue working on the draft after a brief check-in period with Exercise 13, coming up next.

Closing Thoughts

This exercise is perhaps one of the most challenging aspects of your journey, and it may take some time to really drill down to a draft message that is meaningful. Generally speaking, people don't love ruling out options, but they often feel pretty darn good once they do. It is so much easier to move forward with one option than with a hundred. That said, our values continue to evolve AND life has a way of changing and offering up new pathways and opportunities. If you discover you don't like the path you've started working toward, or if things change unforeseeably, you can veer over to a side road that can get you to the same basic place, but in a different way. Or you can start out along a completely new path. You are the driver of your car and get to choose exactly where you want to go!

EXERCISE 13
BRING YOUR VISION INTO FOCUS

At this stage in the process, I would like to help you ensure that

1. The form and scope of the vision goal you're defining are magnetic enough to ensure your level of passion is on point, and

2. Your vision is clear and specific enough to move forward—and if it's not, think about how you can develop it further.

This exercise is designed to take your temperature at this point, to assess where you are at, regarding your thinking about your vision.

Here are a couple of reminders and points to keep in mind while you complete the following exercise:

- A vision's form comprises the "who," "what," and "when" of the goal.
- A vision's scope is determined by its size, in terms of how many people are involved, the potential for impact on others, the number of elements making up the vision, and how they connect.

- For many people completing this exercise, the vision form's "who" will be related to their personal vision for themselves. There may still be an impact on others; however, certain questions may not be as relevant to answer where scope is not a significant factor. (I've added "if relevant" to the test statements below to remind you to think about whether it is or is not for you.)

- Most people start with a small-scope personal vision, but it can morph over time to embrace a broader scope. This was indeed my own experience. Also, do you remember the main character in the movie *Baby Boom* making all those containers of "Country Baby" food for her child? She had a vision of living a healthier life in the country and started making the baby food out of necessity, but eventually ended up selling it locally, then nationally ... this is a great example of re-visioning in motion!

On a scale of 1 to 7, rate yourself on each of the statements in the following five tests.

Record the test titles and your respective ratings in your notebook.

Definitely Not		Definitely Yes
Strongly DISAGREE	Neutral	Strongly AGREE
1 · · · · 2 · · · · 3 · · · ·	4 · · · · 5 · · · ·	6 · · · · 7

TEST 1
HOW PASSIONATE ARE YOU ABOUT YOUR VISION?

1. My vision's **form** (who, what, when) is:
   a) Important to me
   b) Attractive to me
   c) Desirable to me

2. My vision's **scope** (size) is:
   a) Important to me
   b) Attractive to me
   c) Desirable to me

To help you really dial in, consider these additional questions:

- What specific aspects of your vision goal's form and scope feel the most important, attractive, and desirable to you?

- How might you enhance these specific aspects of form and scope to make them even more salient?

- Are there some aspects you still feel wishy-washy about? Can you tighten these up, or possibly remove them or substitute in something that feels better?

- Is there anything you feel is missing and should be added to make the vision more magnetic for you?

TEST 2
HOW CLEAR IS YOUR VISION'S FORM?

At this stage of my vision's development, I feel that it is **clear**:

a) Who, besides me, is involved

b) If others are involved, who they are and how they help facilitate the goal (if relevant)

c) What enacting the vision looks like in my mind

d) What key features or elements make up the goal

e) How separate features or elements relate to one another

f) What the environment in which the goal is enacted looks like

g) What elements of timing are critical to making it happen (for example, is there a required completion date?)

TEST 3
HOW SPECIFIC IS YOUR VISION'S FORM?

At this stage of my vision's development, I feel that the **form** is:

a) Clear

b) Tangible (e.g., easy to visualize)

c) Specific

d) Able to provide direction to others (if relevant)

TEST 4
HOW CLEAR IS YOUR VISION'S SCOPE?

At this stage of my vision's development, I feel that it is **clear**:

a) Who this vision applies to (related to size—me only or others as well)

b) How many other potential people this goal might apply to (if relevant)

c) The extent to which the goal has the potential to help society or contribute to a better future for others (if relevant)

d) How much potential the goal has to create value for myself

e) How much potential the goal has to create value for others (if relevant)

f) Whether there is profit potential (if relevant)

g) How long (days, months, years) it will take to enact (if relevant)

TEST 5
HOW SPECIFIC IS YOUR VISION'S SCOPE?

At this stage of my vision's development, I feel that the **scope** is:

a) Clear

b) Tangible (e.g., easy to visualize)

c) Specific

d) Able to provide direction to others (if relevant)

Here are some additional clarification questions for you to consider:

- Which aspects of your vision feel most clear to you?
- On the other hand, which aspects still don't feel clear enough?
- Can you make a plan for those aspects requiring further clarification by finding out the information required or enlisting the help of others?
- Do you find yourself responding that there is no end date for the timing related to the goal—that it is ongoing and will always be a goal? This may mean that your vision is one with strong purpose and will always help guide you in making other, shorter-term goals.

How Can You Apply What You've Learned Here?

The next exercise, number 14, asks you to return to the draft vision statement that you worked on in Exercise 12. Use your responses from the above scale and clarification questions to help refine your concept and draft. If there are elements of what you were initially focusing on or considering including that you want to remove, feel free to do so! Even if you think something is cool, but it doesn't truly resonate with you for whatever reason, it's time to say bye-bye! Or, if you're not sure, put it on a shelf for "maybe later," but take it out of your draft for now. It's time to get down to brass tacks!

Closing Thoughts

As Ruth Saw notes in *Clarity Is Power*: "Like a diamond, the more clarity we have, the more value we bring."[55]

EXERCISE 14
CREATE YOUR VISION STATEMENT

Today, your aim is to refine the core message of your vision to its essence. This means stripping it down to convey only that value which you aim to deliver to yourself and/or others with this vision.

The value proposition—what your vision offers, whether you're looking to give back to other people or to realize your own fulfillment—is *the* central tenet of any vision-setting exercise. It is mission-critical to fulfilling the promises you make to yourself and others and serves as the basis for your legacy.

> **Polish your draft core message from Exercises 12 and 13.**

1. Shorten your one to three sentences or phrases down to just one sentence (considering refinements you've decided on with input from the previous exercises). Remove any extra words such as "I aim to" or "My goal is to." Start with a verb or verb phrase, an action word that jumps straight in.

2. Shorten that sentence even further—if possible, to no more than seven words. (On average, that is the biggest chunk of information most people can keep in their working memory!) Every word counts and should have high meaning that conveys the core aspects of the value proposition you want to deliver through your vision.

In converting your aspiration to a vision statement, you will find that clarity and simplicity facilitate bringing the vision to fruition. Keep it short and sassy to clearly voice the essence of the value behind your vision.

Here are some well-known, succinct examples of effective and successful vision statements to get your aspirational creative juices flowing:

- Julia Child: "To expand people's awareness of cooking."[56]
- David Suzuki Foundation: "Act every day on the understanding that we are one with nature."[57]
- Oxfam International: "The future is equal."[58]

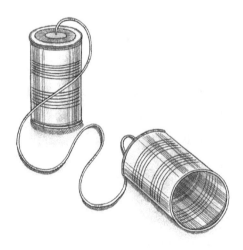

FROM 17 WORDS TO 6

In doing this exercise myself, I had whittled down my purpose to:

Making the path and process of how to be inspired to create vision accessible to the mainstream.

Here are the steps I took to further clarify my vision statement and, in doing so, construct the one that would drive my re-visioned retirement:

1. I wanted to make the abstract concept of "making ... accessible" simpler and clearer. I wanted to do this by replacing the abstract language with a clear image. I decided to just use the word "lighting."
2. The words "how to be inspired," while important, were similarly abstract, and for me the word "lighting" enveloped this idea. The word was an image-rich way of bringing meaning to what I wanted to say using the visual concept of bringing something to light.
3. I felt that the words "path and process" were somehow redundant. Again, the word "path" was image-rich, so I kept only that one word.

Continued...

4. The phrase "the mainstream" was a little complex and jargony and could easily be replaced with the word "all," especially because I did essentially believe that the ability to construct a vision was something that should be accessible to everyone. I also wanted the focus to be about giving back and creating meaning for others by introducing them to the how-to behind visioning.
5. Finally, I was still at eight words and wanted it to be seven or fewer. Since "to see" was somewhat redundant with the idea of lighting for all, I removed it.

As such, my stripped-down, more image-rich, long-term vision statement moving forward became six words:

Lighting the vision path for all.

How Can You Apply What You've Learned Here?

A simple, clear version of your vision statement will enable you to repeat it easily to yourself as an affirmation and communicate it to others.

Closing Thoughts

In the next exercise we will take a final step toward making your vision achievable!

EXERCISE 15
LAY DOWN YOUR FIRST STEPPING STONE

It's time to sweep up all of these great ideas you've been developing on paper and in your mind to begin moving toward your long-term vision. As we saw, way back at the beginning of this workbook, your long-term vision is only part of the picture. While your long-term vision represents a large-scale goal and relates to your aspirational self, you still need to find a place to start. That usually involves shorter-term visions that act as stepping stones to help get you there.

Setting shorter-term vision goals doesn't mean you're letting go of your longer-term vision. It's just that you need to start somewhere. I suggest looking at shorter-term, vision-related opportunities that seem readily doable from the get-go. There's nothing better than an early "win" and proof of the viability of your vision, both for yourself and for others who will be impacted by it, to keep you moving toward your longer-term vision.

Today, we dive into the dynamic world of short-term visions and how they can help cobble a path toward achieving bigger, overarching, longer-term dreams. There are two parts to this exercise.

> **Reflect on a successful short-term vision you've had in your life.**

1. Write down a short-term vision goal you successfully enacted in the past and which truly moved the needle for you.
2. List five things that you feel contributed to that particular short-term vision success story—if possible, prioritize them based on impact or timing.
3. Compare your success ingredients to the following examples from my own list when doing this exercise:

   - Aligning my long-term intentions with my core values
   - Clarifying the long-term goal to "backcast" the necessary steps for reaching it (backcasting is a planning method that starts with defining a desirable future and then works backwards)
   - Setting up initial wins for momentum
   - Enlisting support by vocalizing my intentions to friends, family, and my network
   - Achieving a first stepping stone that unveiled complementary and further steps

> **Set your first short-term vision toward your future.**

The last success ingredient which I noted above is probably the key piece of advice I can offer you at this stage. Find a beachhead—something small that allows you to get started, that allows you to test out how your longer-term vision might be achieved. The idea is to act on a more limited basis—over a shorter time frame, with a smaller group of people, involving fewer resources—to carve out a piece of the bigger puzzle that makes sense to do first. Consider feedback from your visioning team and anyone involved in your beachhead efforts as you continue to refine your dream. Creating shorter-term visions helps springboard you to the enactment of your longer-term vision.

1. Jot down five potential short-term yet meaningful goals that can move you toward where you want to be in the future.

2. Choose one of those goals that has the potential to be highly doable within the next year and that you feel passionate enough about to pursue as a short-term vision.

3. Using the techniques set out in Pillar 3, flesh out this goal by writing a core message describing your short-term vision.

4. Create one sentence that captures that short-term vision.

Tapping into Past Success

After my retirement epiphany, when I decided my vision was to bring value to the newly and about-to-be retired (you!), I was looking for a first small step, a place to start. I enjoy writing and had been working on a book for entrepreneurs about how to develop an A-to-Z vision (*Entrepreneurial Vision*). The research and work I had done provided a meaningful segue from the business world to the group of people I wanted to reach through this book on re-visioning retirement. I was able to use the core visioning concepts and processes I had already created to build a brand-new framework for the NARLYs. The next step was to run a focus group to see whether there was interest in my process, and there definitely was! I learned a lot from the research I did and kept going back to the drawing board to learn more about this new focal point for my vision work. This book offers you the first fruits of this vision.

SUSAN REID

CLOSING THOUGHTS

Congratulations! By creating a first tangible stepping stone, you are now on the way to achieving your longer-term vision!

ENJOY
The Journey

I GENUINELY HOPE THAT GOING THROUGH THIS FUN Re-Visioning process has provided you with some insights and inspiration for moving forward on your retirement path!

I believe that FUN Re-Visioning will open a new door for you. Once you step through, though, things will be different. You will realize your path is not set in stone. You surge forward, move back a little, and hopefully continue to move in the general direction of your aspirations guided by the compass of your values, your intuition, and the guidance of others. This is proactive intention in motion. Just as Alice jumped down the rabbit hole, pursuing this journey does involve a leap of faith—not once, but every day.

Once you have achieved a first short-term goal related to your longer-term vision, look back at your list of five short-term goals from Exercise 15. Is there another one you desire to tackle? Are there others that have popped up that you didn't initially think of to help you on your way? Continue adding these to your list of shorter-term goals, refining and re-visioning as you go. In many ways, the hardest parts are done—you have a clear aspiration in front of you, and you know how the process works if and when you decide to change or add to it. Every time you do it, you will get better at it, too. It will get easier, more natural, and more exciting as all the pieces come into closer alignment between your authentic and aspirational selves.

You are the author of your journey into an ideal future you create in your mind. You have a choice for your path. This doesn't mean it's easy. It's not always possible. But following the path you choose, even if you never reach a specific destination, is truly the most important thing. The path *is* the destination.

It is vision which brings us to the best of ourselves, even if we are never able to enact it fully. Freud notes that "the dream is the liberation of the spirit from the pressure of external nature, a detachment of the soul from the fetters of matter."[59]

As you continue to define your vision, and as it evolves and takes shape—and perhaps gets renewed and re-visioned as you continue to move forward—you are connecting with yourself and others. You are doing the work to learn about your higher purpose, the essence of what you stand for—and now it's time to let your North Star light the path to long-term success.

Happy Travels!

Endnotes

[1] *Cambridge Dictionary*, "retirement," accessed November 8, 2024, https://dictionary.cambridge.org/dictionary/english/retirement.

[2] OECD/European Commission, "Seniors' Self-Employment and Entrepreneurship Activities," in *The Missing Entrepreneurs 2021: Policies for Inclusive Entrepreneurship and Self-Employment* (OECD Publishing, 2021), https://doi.org/10.1787/43446d1c-en.

[3] Richard Fry, "Amid the Pandemic, a Rising Share of Older U.S. Adults Are Now Retired," Pew Research Center, November 4, 2021, www.pewresearch.org/fact-tank/2021/11/04/amid-the-pandemic-a-rising-share-of-older-u-s-adults-are-now-retired.

[4] Gabriela Topa, Marco Depolo, and Carlos-Maria Alcover, "Early Retirement: A Meta-Analysis of Its Antecedent and Subsequent Correlates," *Frontiers in Psychology* 8 (January 2018): 1, article 2157, https://doi.org/10.3389/fpsyg.2017.02157.

[5] The term "Great Resignation" is considered to have been coined by Anthony Klotz, Department of Management, Texas A&M University, during an interview with Arianne Cohen: "How to Quit Your Job in the Great Post-Pandemic Resignation Boom," *Bloomberg*, July 8, 2021, www.bloomberg.com/news/articles/2021-05-10/quit-your-job-how-to-resign-after-covid-pandemic.

[6] Joseph Fuller and William Kerr, "The Great Resignation Didn't Start with the Pandemic," *Harvard Business Review*, March 23, 2022, https://hbr.org/2022/03/the-great-resignation-didnt-start-with-the-pandemic.

[7] Goldman Sachs Asset Management, *Retirement Survey & Insights Report 2023: Diving Deeper into the Financial Vortex; A Way Forward* (Goldman Sachs, 2023), 5, www.gsam.com/content/dam/gsam/pdfs/common/en/public/articles/2023/am-retirement-survey-2023.pdf?sa=n&rd=n.

[8] John Letzing, "How Long Will People Live in the Future?," World Economic Forum, July 26, 2021, www.weforum.org/agenda/2021/07/how-long-will-people-live-in-the-future/.

[9] Katharine G. Abraham, Brad Hershbein, and Susan N. Houseman, "Contract Work at Older Ages," *Journal of Pension Economics & Finance* 20, no. 3 (2021): 426–47, https://doi.org/10.1017/S1474747220000098.

[10] Lisa Bannon, "The New Post-60 Career Paths," *Wall Street Journal*, February 6, 2022, www.wsj.com/articles/the-new-post-60-career-paths-11644166740.

[11] Tom Kirkwood, "Why (and How) Are We Living Longer and What Can We Do about It?," McMaster Institute for Research on Aging (MIRA) presentation, Hamilton, Ontario, Canada, May 1, 2018.

[12] Eric S. Kim, Koichiro Shiba, Julia K. Boehm, and Laura D. Kubzansky, "Sense of Purpose in Life and Five Health Behaviors in Older Adults," *Preventive Medicine* 139 (October 2020): article 106172, https://doi.org/10.1016/j.ypmed.2020.106172.

[13] Angelina R. Sutin, Martina Luchetti, and Antonio Terracciano, "Sense of Purpose in Life and Healthier Cognitive Aging," *Trends in Cognitive Sciences* 25, no. 11 (2021): P917–19, https://doi.org/10.1016/j.tics.2021.08.009.

[14] Stephanie Vozza, "Personal Mission Statements of 5 Famous CEOs (and Why You Should Write One Too)," *Fast Company*, February 25, 2014, www.fastcompany.com/3026791/personal-mission-statements-of-5-famous-ceos-and-why-you-should-write-one-too.

[15] P. Ranganath Nayak and John M. Ketteringham, *Breakthroughs! How the Vision and Drive of Innovators in Sixteen Companies Created Commercial Breakthroughs That Swept the World* (Arthur D. Little and Rawson Associates, 1986).

[16] "About Habitat for Humanity," Habitat for Humanity, accessed September 30, 2024, www.habitat.org/about.

[17] Diana Nyad, *Find a Way: The Inspiring Story of One Woman's Pursuit of a Lifelong Dream* (Vintage Books, 2016).

[18] Marie Kondo, *Spark Joy: An Illustrated Master Class on the Art of Organizing and Tidying Up* (Ten Speed Press, 2016), 8.

[19] Jackie Roberge, "Five Ps to Make Life-Enhancing Changes," in *Power to Change: Top Experts Share Their Powerful Secrets* (Thrive Publishing, 2011).

[20] Daniel W. Rasmus, "Defining Your Company's Vision," *Fast Company*, February 28, 2012, www.fastcompany.com/1821021/defining-your-companys-vision.

[21] Jim Collins and Jerry I. Porras, *Built to Last: Successful Habits of Visionary Companies* (Harper Business, 1994).

[22] James C. Collins and Jerry I. Porras, "Organizational Vision and Visionary Organizations," *California Management Review* 34, no. 1 (1991): 42, https://doi.org/10.2307/41166682.

[23] Paula Span, "Ageism: A 'Prevalent and Insidious' Health Threat," *New York Times*, April 26, 2019, www.nytimes.com/2019/04/26/health/ageism-elderly-health.html.

[24] Marie McNiven, from e-mail correspondence (with permission), January 25, 2024.

[25] Eckhart Tolle, *The Power of Now: A Guide to Spiritual Enlightenment* (Namaste Publishing and New World Library, 1997).

[26] Michael A. Singer, *The Surrender Experiment: My Journey into Life's Perfection* (Harmony Books, 2015), 133.

[27] See, for example, an elaboration of this story by Susan E. Reid and Charles B. Crawford in *Entrepreneurial Vision* (Springer Nature, 2022), 82–83.

[28] Quote from a working session with Jackie Roberge, purpose coach, summer 2024.

[29] Simon Sinek, *Start with Why: How Great Leaders Inspire Everyone to Take Action* (Penguin Books, 2011).

[30] Shalom H. Schwartz, "Understanding Values: Schwartz Theory of Basic Values," *Integration and Implementation Insights: A Community Blog and Repository of Resources for Improving Research Impact on Complex Real-World Problems*, May 10, 2022, https://i2insights.org/2022/05/10/schwartz-theory-of-basic-values/.

[31] William J. Attenweiler and DeWayne Moore, "Goal Orientations: Two, Three, or More Factors?," *Educational and Psychological Measurement* 66, no. 2 (2006): 342, https://doi.org/10.1177/0013164405282473.

[32] Excerpted with permission of Elsevier from Scott B. Button, John E. Mathieu, and Dennis M. Zajac, "Goal Orientation in Organizational Research: A Conceptual and Empirical Foundation," *Organizational Behavior and Human Decision Processes* 67, no. 1 (1996): 33, https://doi.org/10.1006/obhd.1996.0063.

[33] R. Schwarzer and M. Jerusalem, "Generalized Self-Efficacy Scale," in *Measures in Health Psychology: A User's Portfolio (Causal and Control Beliefs)*, eds. J. Weinman, S. Wright, and M. Johnston (NFER-Nelson, 1995), 35–37.

[34] Excerpted from Gilad Chen, Stanley M. Gully, and Dov Eden, "Validation of a New General Self-Efficacy Scale," *Organizational Research Methods* 4, no. 1 (2001): 79, https://journals.sagepub.com/doi/abs/10.1177/109442810141004. Used with permission of Sage Journals under the short excerpts category (<200 words), https://us.sagepub.com/en-us/nam/pre-approved-permission-requests-journals.

[35] Aaron T. Beck, "Cognitive Therapy of Depression: New Perspectives," in *Treatment of Depression: Old Controversies and New Approaches*, eds. Paula J. Clayton and James E. Barrett (Raven Press, 1983).

[36] Excerpted from Peter J. Bieling, Aaron T. Beck, and Gregory K. Brown, "The Sociotropy-Autonomy Scale: Structure and Implications," *Cognitive Therapy and Research* 24, no. 6 (2000): 772, https://doi.org/10.1023/A:1005599714224. Used with permission of Springer Nature (https://link.springer.com/journal/10608) via Copyright Clearance Center, Inc., license granted October 2, 2024.

[37] John G. Pallister and Gordon R. Foxall, "Psychometric Properties of the Hurt-Joseph-Cook Scales for the Measurement of Innovativeness," *Technovation* 18, no. 11 (1998): 663, https://doi.org/10.1016/S0166-4972(98)00070-4.

[38] H. Thomas Hurt, Katherine Joseph, and Chester D. Cook, "Scales for the Measurement of Innovativeness," *Human Communication Research* 4, no. 1 (1977): 58–63, https://doi.org/10.1111/j.1468-2958.1977.tb00597.x.

[39] Excerpted with permission of Elsevier Science & Technology Journals from John G. Pallister and Gordon R. Foxall, "Psychometric Properties of the Hurt-Joseph-Cook Scales for the Measurement of Innovativeness," *Technovation* 18, no. 11 (1998): 664, https://doi.org/10.1016/S0166-4972(98)00070-4. Permission conveyed through Copyright Clearance Center, Inc., license granted October 2, 2024.

[40] Excerpted from Thijs Bouman, Linda Steg, and Henk A. L. Kiers, "Measuring Values in Environmental Research: A Test of an Environmental Portrait Value Questionnaire," *Frontiers in Psychology* 9 (April 2018): 4, article 564, https://doi.org/10.3389/fpsyg.2018.00564. Open-Access Journal, CC-BY License.

[41] Many versions of this saying exist, attributed to many different ancient and modern sources. See Quote Investigator, January 10, 2013, https://quoteinvestigator.com/2013/01/10/watch-your-thoughts/.

[42] *The Brittanica Dictionary*, "passion," accessed October 6, 2024, www.britannica.com/dictionary/passion.

[43] Quote from e-mail correspondence with Hope Paterson, personal coach, winter 2024.

[44] Quote from a discussion with Anna Rumin, PhD, and referenced from her forthcoming book "Stories from Your Life: A Workbook to Get You Going." Quote and permission obtained September 9, 2024.

[45] Abraham H. Maslow, "A Theory of Human Motivation," *Psychological Review* 50, no. 4 (1943): 370–96, https://doi.org/10.1037/h0054346.

[46] *Brittanica*, "self-actualization," last updated August 30, 2024, www.britannica.com/science/self-actualization.

[47] Carol S. Dweck, *Mindset: The New Psychology of Success* (Ballantine Books, 2006).

[48] Twyla Tharp, *The Creative Habit: Learn It and Use It for Life* (Simon & Schuster, 2006), 98.

[49] Tharp, *Creative Habit*, 95.

[50] Geshe Michael Roach and Lama Christie McNally, *The Diamond Cutter: The Buddha on Managing Your Business and Your Life*, rev. ed. (Three Rivers Press, 2009), 214.

[51] Paulo Coelho, *The Alchemist* (HarperOne, 2014), 70.

[52] Geshe Michael Roach and Lama Christie McNally, *The Diamond Cutter: The Buddha on Managing Your Business and Your Life*, rev. ed. (Three Rivers Press, 2009).

[53] Roach and McNally, *Diamond Cutter*, "Following Up" epilogue.

[54] Roach and McNally, *Diamond Cutter*, 33.

[55] Ruth Saw, *Clarity Is Power: How to Stop Comparing and Step into Your Personal Authority* (Clarity Expert, 2020), 26.

[56] Kelly A. Spring, "Julia Child," National Women's History Museum, 2017, www.womenshistory.org/education-resources/biographies/julia-child.

[57] "About Us," David Suzuki Foundation, accessed February 3, 2025, https://davidsuzuki.org/about/.

[58] Oxfam International home page, accessed February 3, 2025, www.oxfam.org/en/.

[59] Sigmund Freud, quoting Schubert, in Chapter I of *Dream Psychology: Psychoanalysis for Beginners* (James A. McCann Company, 1921), accessed on Bartleby (published online 2010), https://www.bartleby.com/lit-hub/dream-psychology-psychoanalysis-for-beginners/.

Acknowledgements

I would like to thank and acknowledge the support from several people who have read and provided editing assistance during earlier versions of this book: Charles Crawford, Haley Crawford, Dominic Farrell, Maureen McCarthy, Hope Paterson, and Anna Rumin. I would also like to thank the wonderful people from the Barlow Books family who have made the final book a reality: Sarah Scott, Tracy Bordian, Eleanor Gasparik, Dawn Loewen, and Rob Scanlan, as well as the illustrator, Gillian Reid. The book took its shape and direction from all of these people's close and careful attention. It would not have been the work it became without their involvement. Thank you, all!

About the Author

SUSAN REID is an award-winning expert on the topic of vision. Until 2021, Susan was a professor of marketing and entrepreneurship at Bishop's University in Lennoxville, Quebec. As a teacher, researcher, and keynote speaker, she works at the intersection of marketing, innovation, and user-focused design, with an in-depth focus on the topic of vision, particularly for older adults and entrepreneurs. Susan is also the co-founder of Domaine Pinnacle, a pioneering Canadian producer of craft ciders and spirits.

When she retired at age 57, after years of helping businesses and individuals develop their visions, Susan realized, to her surprise, that she had not set a vision for her own retirement. This led her to develop a workbook for people just like her.

Susan holds a Bachelor of Science degree from Queen's University, an MBA from McGill University, and a Ph.D. from Concordia University's John Molson School of Business.